EXERCISE ALTERNATIVES FOR TRAINING EMERGENCY MANAGEMENT COMMAND CENTER STAFFS

by
Walter G. Green III, Ph.D., CEM

Universal Publishers/uPUBLISH.com
USA • 2000

Exercise Alternatives For
Training Emergency Management Command Center Staffs

Copyright (c) 2000 Walter G. Green III
All Rights Reserved.

Universal Publishers/uPUBLISH.com
USA • 2000

ISBN: 1-58112-748-0

www.upublish.com/books/green2.htm

TABLE OF CONTENTS

LIST OF TABLES

PREFACE

As a working emergency manager who came to the profession as a second career, I have always been fascinated by the combination of high stress and the demand for high reliability performance that disaster response work requires. At the same time, coming from a field of work that demanded monthly, weekly, and even daily drills and exercises, I was surprised by the lack of practice for the inevitable bad event that is engaged in by emergency management systems.

There are good reasons for this. Emergency managers often can only give part of their attention to the business of emergency management. Extricating other key team members from their daily responsibilities for training to prepare for a once every couple of years event is even tougher. And the way exercise design is taught as a process that requires a large expenditure of time and effort contributes to this.

This volume, based on research in a graduate program and field testing in emergency management organizations, is an attempt to give emergency managers tools to make exercising easier, faster, cheaper, and, most importantly, more frequent. We can only be prepared to protect our citizens when we practice our essential tasks, individually, in small teams, and as a system, often enough so that everyone can find the emergency operations center and knows how to use it.

I would like to dedicate this study to a Springer Spaniel named Snickers, a much loved and missed companion and friend, who kept me company through the original project.

Glen Allen, Virginia, February 2000

I. INTRODUCTION

Looking for Alternatives

What alternatives are available to provide low cost options, in time, personnel, and funding, for training emergency management personnel in decision making in response to disasters? An existing system of five exercise types has developed over the past thirty years to provide a continuum of options for exercise training. However, practices in other emergency fields, and in the armed forces, suggest that other exercise models may provide inexpensive and effective exercise training to supplement the standard progression of Orientation, Tabletop, Drill, Functional, and Full Scale Exercises.

Background

Emergency management is "an organized effort to mitigate against, prepare for, respond to, and recover from an emergency" (US FEMA EMI 1989c, 1-6). As a governmental function, emergency management fulfills a critical coordination role in protecting the citizens from the effects of disasters. Operationally, the tasks involved are performed by a mix of paid and volunteer personnel who work for both primary response agencies, such as fire departments and emergency medical services agencies, and a wide variety of support organizations. These organizations routinely do emergency work; these day-to-day responses are termed routine emergencies to distinguish them from major disasters (Hoetmer 1991, xvii). However, they rarely operate as part of a large-scale community response to disasters in an integrated

1

emergency management system.

To prepare to perform as part of an integrated team, officials with emergency management jobs must be trained in their specific duties. Intuitively we can classify emergency management training, as delivered today, as falling into four broad categories:

1.   Individual--Self-Directed Learning: Emergency management independent study courses (US FEMA EMI 1995b) have long been offered. However, the definition of self-directed learning is broader, "a training design in which trainees master packages of predetermined material, at their own pace, without the aid of an instructor" (Piskurich 1993, 4). This definition extends beyond the traditional correspondence, extension, or independent study course used to deliver emergency management self-directed learning. If self-directed learning is to be taken in its broadest sense, the potential exists for the design and use of self-directed exercises an individual can complete on his or her own for training in some types of emergency management skills.

2.   Individual--Classroom Training: Classroom training is a standard means of preparing emergency managers to do their jobs. In 1995 the Emergency Management Institute, the Federal Emergency Management Agency's technical college, presented 41 in-residence courses, with 67 more being available through state emergency management departments (US FEMA EMI 1995b). A cursory examination of the 2000 Catalog shows changes in emphasis and an increase in Independent Study options, but it reflects overall a similar level of effort (US FEMA EMI 1999). The role of classroom training is central to preparing the emergency manager for improved performance on the job (House 1996, 439), even if only because

of the size of the current effort. Exercises can provide a valid method to expand the presentation options for the emergency management instructor.

3.   Team: In most emergency operations, teams are the standard work unit, implying that training of teams must have a high priority (DeVito 1996, 89). In fire departments the team structure is obvious--fire companies, the basic organizational unit of an officer, two to four firefighters, and a vehicle, are teams. However, emergency operations center staffs also have team structures, composed of representatives of a standard list of agencies, many of whom know each other well through their other contacts in government. Although team members may attend classroom training together, training for teams in working as a team is primarily delivered through exercises. The majority of these events are local, state, and national exercises conducted in the ways described in this volume. However, the Federal Emergency Management Agency and at least two states conduct integrated emergency management exercises as courses with a full staff from either a local jurisdiction (US FEMA EMI 1995b, 23) or a state (National Voluntary Organizations Active in Disaster 1996, 5). For example, the Virginia Department of Emergency Services conducts a Local Emergency Management Operations Course for local jurisdictions, combining two days of classroom training with a day-long exercise for employees, from executives to clerical staff.

4.   System: August Smith (1982, 3) defines a system as "a set of entities that interact." In the emergency management context systems include, as their entities, response agencies, their equipment, command centers, communications, the media, and the public. Systems training depends primarily on exercises which involve actual field problems. Although

3

these would seem to offer the most realistic system training, other exercise types may also involve nearly complete system participation.

This discussion highlights the need for an effective exercise program. In a broad sense an exercise is a structured simulation of reality for the purpose of training, evaluating, testing, or planning. A wide variety of events may legitimately be called exercises, drills, wargames, or simulations. These terms often are used interchangeably or even in a contradictory manner. However, this study specifically focuses on types of exercises used to train command center staffs and test plans and procedures, without requiring the actual use of operational facilities or the participation of response resources in the field.

Command centers are facilities from which emergency operations are directed. Such facilities may range in size and complexity from portable brief case units, through vehicle configurations, to permanent work areas in buildings. The smaller and more portable or mobile versions of these are typically called command posts and are designed for the direction of field operations by incident commanders at the scene of the emergency (Brunacini 1985, 212). The Fire Department of the City of New York uses a large folding board mounted on a tripod as the central focus of its fire command posts (Front Cover September/October 1995). Mobile command posts range from purpose-built modules inserted into the back of a Chevrolet Suburban to large vehicles on van, bus, or motor home frames (Larson September/October 1995).

The larger, fixed facilities are emergency operations centers (EOC) responsible for coordinated management of a jurisdiction's response (Bahme 1978, 40-41 and Carlson 1983, 12). The emergency operations center's key roles include

4

direction, control, and warning. These roles are carried out more efficiently when key officials and their support staffs are located in the same facility (US FEMA 1984, Introduction). Command centers typically are furnished with work stations, communications systems, displays, and reference materials required to direct operations. These centers may be staffed by a full range of personnel, including organizational executives, managers and supervisors, and support, administrative, and clerical personnel (Perry 1991, 208).

Command centers perform a central role in the management of emergency response operations. Regardless of the mission assigned to an organization, the center provides the ability for managers to mobilize people and equipment, determine the situation, accept taskings, direct operations, and report results (Perry 1991, 204-205). At the state level, a state emergency operations center (EOC) coordinates state level disaster response. For example, in the Commonwealth of Virginia, the Virginia Emergency Operations Center coordinates the unified response of all state agencies and serves as a link between local and federal response management (COVA DES 1991, 8). Similarly, local jurisdiction EOCs provide facilities for the management of local response (US FEMA EMI 1993, 1-14).

State government departments may also operate specialized emergency command centers. The Virginia Department of Transportation staffs a sophisticated, computer based Transportation EOC 24 hours a day to manage both day-to-day and emergency highway operations. This facility is unique in Virginia in its 24 hour operations staffing; other agencies and local jurisdictions have 24 hour communications staffing, but only bring their operations sections to 24 hour staffing as disasters threaten. For example, crisis assignments

5

to the Department of Military Affairs are passed from the Virginia EOC to the Virginia State Area Command EOC for tasking to individual National Guard units (COVA DMA ARNG 1992, 3). The Virginia Department of Health operates an Emergency Support Center to coordinate response by state agencies and emergency medical services task forces (COVA DH OEMS 1996a). Neither of these facilities are continuously staffed.

This range of command centers provides a continuum of management for emergency operations. Policy and coordination issues are worked at state and local EOCs, with a focus on providing resources and policy direction needed to solve the problem. On-scene operations are directed from field command posts as part of the incident command or management system used for directing on-scene operations with the objective of controlling the emergency situation and limiting the damage.

The effective operation of any command center depends on a well trained staff that understands its duties and is capable of functioning as a team. The importance of EOC staff training was demonstrated by its selection as the topic for the course planning exercise by 8 of 23 students in a 24-28 June 1996 offering of Course E603 Instructional Design at the Emergency Management Institute, Emmitsburg, Maryland. The student mix included both experienced state and county level emergency management training officers, highlighting the criticality of EOC training at all levels of operations management.

The role of exercises as a training tool for state and local government command center staffs has been recognized by the Federal Emergency Management Agency. In the EOC's

Management and Operations Course, exercises are specifically identified as improving coordination, clarifying roles and responsibilities, and improving individual performance (US FEMA EMI 1995c, 3-77). This is not just a theoretical relationship; exercises are integral to such other courses as the Emergency Operations Center--Incident Command System Interface Workshop (with two exercises included in 11 hours of training) (US FEMA EMI 1993).

The State of the Art in Emergency Management Exercises

The evolution of emergency management exercises has resulted in a tightly integrated and coherent approach to exercise design and conduct at the local, state, and federal levels. The Federal Emergency Management Agency has developed and advocated a standard set of five disaster exercises as shown in summary form in Table 1.

This system serves as a de facto benchmark for any effort to develop emergency management exercises because of its status as a standard within the profession. This status has been reinforced by two important mechanisms, instruction in how to conduct exercises in training courses and previous criteria for Federal funding.

The Federal Emergency Management Agency provides significant training support to states and local jurisdictions in their efforts to develop effective exercise programs. In the early 1990s the Emergency Management Institute's curriculum was changed to include a 40 hour, state delivered Exercise Design Course as part of the seven course Professional Development Series (US FEMA EMI 1995b, 40). Incorporation of this training in the Professional Development Series demonstrates

7

Table 1.
Federal Emergency Management Agency Exercise Types

	Orientation	Tabletop
Format	lecture or seminar discussion based on a scenario	seminar discussion with problems interjected by message
Objective	train staff on new plans or procedures	train staff on plans; test plans and procedures; develop resource allocations; assign roles
Time	1-2 hours	1-4 hours
Participants	any staff	usually key staff and supervisors
Facilities	conference or classroom	conference room
Stress Level	no stress	low stress
Frequency	as needed	as needed

Notes: Times are estimates based on observed exercises. Frequency reflects 1993 requirements for Emergency Management Assistance funding--there is no current federal requirement for exercise frequency.

Table 1 - continued

	Drill	Functional
Format	practice by a part of an agency or system in use of actual equipment	practice by a function of the system in the use of full procedures and facilities
Objective	train staff in actual hands-on equipment use	train functional staff in use of actual procedures under more realistic conditions
Time	1-4 hours	1-8 hours
Participants	field responders	all personnel assigned to a specific function
Facilities	field practice area with full equipment	actual facility with standard forms, plans, displays, computers, communications
Stress Level	moderate	moderate
Frequency	as needed	three times in four years

Notes: Function refers to a specific area of response operations, such as fire fighting, mass care, or command and control.

9

Table 1 - continued

	Full Scale
Format	complete simulated emergency with movement of actual resources to solve physical problems
Objective	train entire system in emergency response operations; provide a realistic test of plans and procedures matched against resources
Time	3 hours to 10 days
Participants	all levels from responders through chief executive
Facilities	all those used in actual responses
Stress Level	moderate to high
Frequency	once every four years

Source: United States, Federal Emergency Management Agency, Emergency Management Institute (1989), Exercise Design Course: Student Workbook, Washington, DC, U. S. Government Printing Office, 20-21.

the importance of exercises as a component of emergency management course knowledge. This sequence of courses served for many years as essentially a professional certification program for emergency managers.

A second state delivered course, the Exercise Evaluation Course, was developed to improve how exercise results were used in communities (US FEMA EMI 1992, ii). In addition, an Independent Study course, An Orientation to Community Disaster Exercises, was introduced in 1995 to make basic information readily available to anyone interested in how to construct and conduct effective exercises (US FEMA EMI 1995a).

In 1999 a major enhancement in exercise training, the Master Exercise Practitioner Program, was announced in the Emergency Management Institute catalog. This new combination of eight courses and a practicum is intended to "establish a level of professional achievement and recognition for persons charged with administering and conducting emergency management exercise programs and activities" (US FEMA EMI 1999, 7). As such it parallels the already established Master Trainer Program as a source for individuals thoroughly trained in the Federal Emergency Management Agency's exercise philosophy.

However, standardized training is only part of the reason for the common approach to exercises. The second component was a previous requirement for exercise activity as a precondition for Federal funding under the Emergency Management Assistance program. This included reporting of three types of exercises in the Emergency Management Exercise Reporting System: Tabletop, Functional, and Full Scale (US FEMA 1993). Under this program, specific types of

11

exercises had to be conducted on a set schedule. Although the Emergency Management Exercise Reporting System appears to no longer be operational, and the funding requirement has lapsed, it seems reasonable to assume that experienced emergency managers will still gauge exercise requirements by their earlier experiences.

This background suggests that alternatives to the existing structure of standard approaches established by the Federal Emergency Management Agency will have to offer significant benefits in order to be attractive. Simply not fitting the established model may be enough to disqualify an option.

In addition, narrowness of viewpoint exists in emergency management, much as it does in other professions. During a medical Tabletop Exercise conducted by the Virginia Office of Emergency Medical Services, one participant, a Certified Emergency Manager, stated that the exercise was the worst he had ever participated in because it was impossible to hold an exercise without a specific emergency operations plan. The stated objective of the exercise was to capture current practices in order to develop options for inclusion in a new plan (COVA DH OEMS 1995b). The result more than satisfied the objective, with 141 items developed (COVA DH OEMS 1995a), most of which were incorporated in a new Health and Medical Annex to the Virginia Emergency Operations Plan (COVA DES 1996).

Therefore, new exercise types potentially require an additional investment in training to ensure their appropriate use. And new exercise types need to enhance the existing continuum, providing additional opportunities for progressive training for organizations and personnel assigned emergency management duties.

II. CONCEPTS FOR STRUCTURING EXERCISE TRAINING

Issues in Progressive Training

An exercise program should provide command center personnel a structured series of learning events. Commonly accepted principles of adult learning hold that training should build from the known to the unknown and from the simple to the complex. In 1984 Morentz recognized this principle by developing a structured and logical sequence of exercises, from Orientation to Full Scale. In addition, the Federal Emergency Management Agency emphasizes a progressive exercise program, defining these terms as:

"Progressive" in that one exercise builds upon another.

A "program," in that it is a carefully planned sequence that will meet specified goals .... (US FEMA EMI 1995a, 8)

Research in andragogy emphasizes adult learning factors that make exercises an important teaching tool. Adults have a broad base of experience which can serve as the foundation for further experiential learning. Techniques which capitalize on this resource, including those which are hands-on and participative, are highly effective. Knowledge and skills are more easily added to the experience base when a building block approach progresses from the old, simple, and known to the new and more complex (Knowles and Hartl 1995, 217-218).

This suggests that a progressive exercise program can be structured to exploit how emergency management practitioners could be expected to learn most effectively. Increasingly complex exercises emphasize greater involvement, more and advanced functional skills, and broadened experience in a variety of scenarios. This instructional strategy should provide trainers a clear sequence of exercise types to meet training needs at all levels of the organization.

However, the existing FEMA model of exercise types does not offer a gradual progression. There are significant differences between an Orientation Exercise and a Tabletop, a Tabletop and a Functional Exercise, and a Functional and a Full Scale Exercise. As a result, each exercise type requires significant adjustments by participants when making a transition to a new level.

One example of these differences in complexity, for decision making, is summarized in Table 2. The transition required from the Tabletop to the Functional Exercise is particularly sharp. The individual is expected to move from group consensus decisions in a conference room under little pressure to an individual decision making process under the considerable pressure of operating with actual systems and facilities. With experienced participants who are primarily working on team building or the understanding of specific procedures this would not seem to be a problem.

However, for personnel new to command centers, changes in more than one dimension of complexity and difficulty potentially can overwhelm the participant and limit learning. To use a simple example, it is very difficult to concentrate on making decisions about which shelters to open if you cannot figure out how to make the phone system work.

14

Table 2.
Differences in Decision Making in Federal Emergency
Management Agency Exercises

Exercise Type	Decision Characteristics	
Orientation	no decisions required	
Tabletop	(1)	group decisions
	(2)	low pressure
	(3)	minimal documentation of decisions
	(4)	minimal resource constraints
	(5)	minimal consideration of time and distance
	(6)	no technology
Functional	(1)	individual (in role) or coordinated decisions
	(2)	increased pressure
	(3)	written documentation of decisions
	(4)	some resource constraints
	(5)	some consideration of time and distance
	(6)	some use of supporting technology (computers, radios, etc.)

Table 2 - continued

Exercise Type	Decision Characteristics	
Full Scale	(1)	individual decisions with some coordination
	(2)	medium to high pressure
	(3)	documentation may depend on supporting staff but must be complete
	(4)	real resources
	(5)	real time and distance
	(6)	actual technology

Therefore, when using progressive exercise training, the exercise designer should consider using models that allow variation in exercise characteristics based on participant experience levels.

In this context, the impact of the new personnel cohort in staffing an emergency operations center (EOC) should not be underestimated. In 1996 two jurisdictions at the edge of the Washington, DC, commuter area in Virginia conducted Local Emergency Management Operations Exercises. In one case the County Emergency Management Coordinator estimated that 90 percent of the staff of the EOC had not worked in a command center prior to the exercise. A survey of the staff in the second jurisdiction indicated that 85 percent of the participants had no prior EOC experience. This is not a criticism of these localities--rather it represents reality in much of the country.

Structuring to Train in Critical Functions

The existing Federal Emergency Management Agency system of exercises has addressed perceived needs in training to perform critical duties within a command center. New alternatives must be capable of addressing the same functions. This requires that we be able to identify the key roles of command centers and assess the performance of alternatives in these areas. Discussions of the functions of fireground command posts and emergency operations centers suggests that the key functions shown in Table 3 are representative.

As noted in the table, the great majority of possible functions would seem to be suitable for incorporation in any type of command center exercise. The role of the command post differs from that of the emergency operations center in breadth of area covered and in the number and level of functions performed. However, with the exception of policy making, most of the functions that could be simulated in an exercise are common to both facilities.

Increasing Flexibility

Alternative approaches to exercises should provide increased flexibility in delivery strategies. An increased variety of exercise models would allow training to be delivered in a larger variety of settings. Descriptions of Orientation and Tabletop Exercises are very specific in describing the types of facilities that should be used as exercise sites. In both cases, the clear preference is for conference room settings (US FEMA EMI 1989b, 20). Alternative exercise designs should allow training in office settings, at home, as part of other instructional presentations, on the Internet, etc.

17

Table 3.
Key Functions of Command Centers

Command Post	Emergency Operations Center
coordination*	coordination*
……….	policy making*
……….	operations management*
communications*	communications*
direction of tactical operations*	……….
predictable location for command	central location for government
view of incident area	……….
collection of situation information*	all types of information gathering*
incident documentation*	incident documentation*
……….	record keeping*
public information*	public information*
	hosting visitors*

Note: Items marked with an asterisk appear to be appropriate for and capable of inclusion in command center exercises.

Sources: Alan V. Brunacini (1985), Fire Command, Quincy, MA, National Fire Protection Association, 212. Ronny J. Coleman (1978), Management of Fire Services Operations, Boston, MA, Breton Publishers, 122. Ronald W. Perry (1991), "Managing Disaster Response Operations," in Emergency Management: Principles and Practice for Local Government, Thomas E. Drabek and Gerard J. Hoetmer, editors, Washington, DC, International City Management Association, 204.

Secondly, exercise training should be conducted both in groups (the traditional model of team training) and for individuals. The addition of self-directed learning exercises makes it possible to provide individual training when that is desirable. If exercises are designed to be capable of being used in either role, it would seem to increase assurance that participants will all receive the same type of training.

Finally, exercise training can be conducted either on a schedule or when opportunity permits. Commonly personnel assigned to command center staffs are not employed primarily in this role. The normal staffing pattern is for agencies to actually supply representatives from their staff only for the period of the actual activation of the emergency operations center (COVA DES 1994). Time given to command center training is time away from their main duties. A method that allows individual or small group opportunity training may increase the probability of all personnel having an increased exposure to their duties.

At the same time, training packages that are this flexible

may be of value in conducting just-in-time training prior to a major event. Just-in-time, as a production or service delivery concept, focuses on the delivery of needed materials just prior to their actually being required. As a result, storage and finance costs are reduced. Just-in-time can be adapted to training by providing highly focused job instruction prior to an individual having to perform the tasks for which he or she has been trained. According to the learning principle of recency, this should increase retention when it is most needed.

III. BENCHMARKING AND VALIDITY

Design

This study was intended to identify exercise types that are potentially applicable to emergency management needs based on the applied practice in other emergency response disciplines. The key components in this process were a review of the academic and practitioner literature of exercises, the inspection of extant data and exercise method descriptions, and benchmarking current practices.

Benchmarking

Benchmarking establishes (1) what the best practices in use in any organization are and (2) what other equivalent organizations are doing as their standard practice. It then compares a specific program to the Benchmark (Svenson and Rinderer 1992, 109). As already noted above, the Federal Emergency Management Agency exercise program serves as a standard, and thus as a convenient benchmark.

Based on this standard, I searched for a recognized exemplary exercise program. James Lee Witt, Director of the Federal Emergency Management Agency, defines an exemplary practice in emergency management as "any idea, project, program, technique, or method in emergency management that has worked in one place and may be worthy of adopting elsewhere" (US FEMA 1995, Foreward). A review of the Federal Emergency Management Agency's Partnerships in Preparedness: A Compendium of Exemplary Practices in Emergency Management, Volumes I through III (1995, 1997,

21

1998), showed that not one exercise program was cited as an Exemplary Practice in Emergency Management, from among 152 programs cited as exemplary.

Review of earlier published exemplary practices case studies highlighted one exercise. This program for the North Dakota Boys' State was an annual Table Top exercise designed to familiarize male high school students with the role of government in a disaster (US FEMA EMI 1987). Although interesting as a cultural artifact, this did not provide useful data for examining exercises to train and test operational personnel.

As the second step of benchmarking, I attempted to determine what might be considered an acceptable exercise program. Exercise requirements for emergency management agencies are not demanding. With changes in Federal funding assistance to local government emergency management agencies, there appears to no longer be any general mandated requirement for exercise training. However, as late as 1995, the Federal Emergency Management Agency required agencies that received Emergency Management Assistance funding to conduct four exercises in a four year period. Three of these were Functional Exercises, and one was required to be a Full Scale Exercise involving actual movement of resources (US FEMA EMI 1995a, 5). There was no specific requirement for command center personnel to exercise in their unique tasks.

An examination of course material intended for local emergency managers indicates a much more ambitious schedule for a typical city. One course suggests two Orientation Exercises, two Tabletops, one Drill, one Functional Exercise, and one Full Scale Exercise in a period of between eight and 18 months (US FEMA EMI 1995a, 9-10). When an entire jurisdiction is included, there is a well funded program, and

22

agencies are actively conducting disaster specific training in their own functions, this may be an achievable goal. However, in the majority of cases, anecdotal experience indicates a realistic frequency of less than one exercise a year.

One major source of community disaster exercises is the Federal Aviation Administration's requirement that airports conduct a Full Scale Exercise every three years. Typically these are integrated to test not only the ability of the airport, but also the support the local jurisdictions can provide to a major incident. Some airports also conduct routine Tabletop Exercises in the interim years to maintain some level of proficiency and to test plans (Nunnally 1999).

The Joint Commission on the Accreditation of Healthcare Organizations (JCAHO) (1995, 338) provides a second source of community exercises. JCAHO requires two hospital exercises a year, one of which must be a Full Scale Exercise. It is interesting that the JCAHO effectively discourages the use of Tabletop Exercises by not awarding exercise credit toward accreditation for their use. Instead Joint Commission standards are commonly interpreted as requiring hospitals to primarily use Functional and Full Scale Exercises involving the actual movement of people.

Dr. Norman McSwain commented on the frequency of hospital disaster drills based on lessons learned in the 1991 Persian Gulf War. McSwain reinforces the importance of the training law of recency and rejects the adequacy of the JCAHO's twice a year schedule for preparation of staffs for emergency operations when he says:

> The way to make this work efficiently is to have a drill once a week. I know everyone says that's an

23

impossibility; that may be correct, but if we're going to practice only every 6 months, we have to accept the fact that we're not going to do it well. (Nordberg October 1991, 44)

Another source of exercise requirements is a major volunteer emergency services organization, the Civil Air Patrol. The Civil Air Patrol participates in a significant percentage of search and rescue and disaster response operations conducted in the United States, either in response to state government taskings or in its role as the United States Air Force's auxiliary. The Air Forces requires that Civil Air Patrol conduct two exercises each year in each state, one a graded search and rescue evaluation and one a graded disaster response evaluation. However, both evaluations can be satisfied with a single Full Scale Exercise. Other search and rescue and disaster response exercises may be conducted (Civil Air Patrol 1992, 10), with the number typically depending on available funding.

Finally, I examined exercise practices in a class of organization that has made an effort to create a niche for itself in disaster response. State defense forces are volunteer military organizations that support their state Army National Guards. With the disappearance of their original role of providing Governors a force to replace a federalized National Guard, some of these organizations have shifted their attention to support of the National Guard's state disaster response missions. This parallels increased National Guard interest in specialized disaster response roles (Daigle August 1996).

As a baseline for defense force practice, I reviewed the quarterly publication of the State Guard Association of the United States for the period 1993 through 1995. Two command center exercises were reported during this period. In November

1994 the Maryland Defense Force conducted a one day statewide hurricane exercise ("Maryland: Command Post Exercise Held" Winter 1994, 11). And in 1995 the Alabama State Defense Force conducted a two day command post exercise to simulate a natural disaster ("Alabama: Command Post Exercise Held" Summer/Fall 1995, 6). A request for information on exercises on America On Line's State Military Reserve topic area generated one reply, describing an exercise conducted 14 years ago by the Ohio National Guard staff for the Ohio Military Reserve (Iott December 1995).

Although there was no direct comparison available for benchmarking, I constructed a strawman benchmark as the basis for comparison with common practices already described. This benchmark exercise program called for:

1.   A mix of exercise types designed to progressively train:

a.   individuals in their duties,

b.   command center staffs as teams in the internal functions of the command center, and

c.   command center staffs in their roles in working with field response units and other agencies.

2.   Exercises tied as closely as possible to actual constraints in personnel, communications, and equipment.

3.   Exercise types that allow command center staffs to participate in as many exercises a year as possible.

In reviewing the options for exercise design as part of an

exercise system, I reviewed the literature describing emergency services exercises to identify:

      1.   The types of exercises that might meet needs for command center exercises,

      2.   The procedures for exercise design, and

      3.   Options for conducting exercises.

Included in the review were materials on military, emergency management, hospital, specific emergency response agency functional, and business exercises. Additional perspective was provided through examination of procedures used in structured simulation gaming as applied to hobby wargames. Table 4 suggests common elements that emerged from this review.

Validity

Determining measures of validity for emergency management exercises is difficult because of at least three factors. First, the role of disaster response organizations may vary based on the characteristics of the disaster. As a result the tasks assigned to organizations can change, sometimes substantially, from one disaster to another. Secondly, disasters are infrequent enough events, and vary enough in their characteristics, that it is difficult to predict the efficacy of a particular control measure in a specific event. This makes it difficult to develop reasonable measures of exercise participant efficiency in any given role. Finally, there are many operational measures of validity. Given the nature of exercises, their frequency, and the fluid nature of the participant population, those measures of validity that offer on their face the greatest confidence through the greatest degree of quantification are the

Table 4.
Exercise Evaluation Criteria

Criteria	Demonstrated By
Fits within a progressive program of exercises (Benchmark 1)	(1) provides an incremental change in at least one aspect of complexity (2) does not radically depart from other methods of exercise play (3) simple adaptations can increase level of complexity or stress
Provides increased flexibility of exercise delivery (Benchmark 3)	(1) allows self-directed learning (2) can be used by varying sized groups (3) can be used on relatively short notice (4) allows frequent exercises
Provides team and individual training (Benchmark 1)	(1) can be used by any system emergency response discipline (2) allows team play (3) other components can either play or be simulated

Table 4 - continued

Criteria	Demonstrated By
Provides realistic resource constraints (Benchmark 2)	(1) provides specific resource lists (2) allows resources available to fluctuate during the simulated event
Engages the participants (Benchmark 1)	(1) reasonable degree of realism (2) exercise seen as interesting, or thought provoking

least likely to be usable.

The practitioner literature of disaster exercises does not attempt to address the validity of exercise models and design. In the single reference located, Foster (1980, 128) implied, but did not directly state, that disaster models are valid if they can replicate many of the characteristics of prior disaster events. Extrapolated to exercises, this suggests that an exercise may be valid if the outcome mirrors an actual event, given the same inputs. With this dearth of commentary, I believe it is reasonable to examine the writings of authorities on military wargaming to draw possible parallels. A military wargame has many of the characteristics of a disaster exercise, and disaster responses are typically managed in a paramilitary manner.

Peter Perla (1990, 266-267) stated that "a wargame's validity can be defined as the extent to which its processes and results represent real problems and issues as opposed to artificial ones generated only by the gaming environment." However, he admitted that defining validity is difficult and that even participants may find judging the limits of the validity of a particular wargame challenging. Based on his definition, Perla proposed criteria that may be used to assess the validity of game results. Those that appear applicable to this study include:

1.   Player definitions of game results.

2.   Are models used to define or quantify results.

3.   The influence of starting assumptions in the scenario on results.

4.   The extent to which the game results are controlled by the mechanics of play.

5.   The effect of mathematical models and the input values used by the models on the game.

6.   The impact of unlikely events on player actions and game results.

Alfred H. Hausrath (1971, 292) considered many of the issues posed by Perla and answered the question as to whether wargames give valid answers with the qualifier that "the question is dependent upon whether the model agrees with nature." He suggested that validity is determined by how the model on which the game is based functions. He assessed the validity of the three categories of game models as:

1. For deterministic models (in which the fixed mathematical relationships of the model do not change from one play to the next), validity may be determined with relative certainty.

2. For models for which probabilities for the various events can be determined, the results determined by the model may fall within statistical limits. Hausrath does point out that this is subject to sensitivity analysis (284).

3. In models which are not deterministic and which also do not employ known probability distributions, either the model must be accepted as providing answers of unknown validity or expert judgment must be applied to determine validity (292-293).

In examining validity criteria, I considered Perla's and Hausrath's work and applied three qualifying criteria.

1. Can validity measures be defined that will make sense to average practitioners with a Bachelor's degree?

2. Is it possible to develop validity measures that can be applied easily, requiring no technical skill or detailed analysis by people who have limited time to build and conduct the exercise?

3. Given the evolving environment, are the validity measures good enough? In other words, do they provide a reasonable level of assurance of validity without becoming too expensive in time and effort to justify the cost of incremental improvements?

The procedures used for demonstrating curricular

validity in tests offer a useful perspective in determining the validity of an exercise design. Weiss and Scott (1959, 224) pointed out that, in designing tests, "validity is the degree to which the test fulfills its purpose." If we extend this statement to exercises as tests, in setting up the framework of the exercise, such as the rules and the scenario, the exercise will be valid to the extent to which these elements coincide with the normal characteristics of the scenario event. This requires a careful identification of the sequence of events in a particular type of disaster, considering the historical range of local effects.

Validity is also demonstrated when the exercise elements include all of the components normally found in the emergency response to the event. This requires the exercise design to consider existing plans, agreements, standard operating procedures, and common practice. Ideally the exercise will allow participants to carry out their response as they should (assuming competent player performance). When these elements are present in approximately the same proportion as is found in actual events, validity is enhanced.

Finally, in testing, validity may be demonstrated when it is possible to show that each element is developed using commonly accepted procedures (Weiss and Scott 1959, 224). Procedures used in alternative exercise designs should not deviate significantly from those advocated by Morentz, the Emergency Management Institute, or other authorities without a reasonable explanation.

Weiss and Scott (1959, 245-246) described a second approach to validation of tests, descriptive validity. Descriptive validity requires an explanation of the instrument and a step-by-step logical exposition of how it meets the desired criteria. This includes a careful definition of each component of the exercise.

Based on these considerations, I propose the following tests for validity for command center exercises:

1. Can the exercise be constructed using commonly accepted procedures for defining exercise objectives, key events, and specific inputs?

2. Is there a logical linkage between exercise events and exercise objectives? Do the events support the objectives?

3. Does the exercise replicate the sequence and character of events that would be found in an actual emergency situation? Are the expected components of the emergency found in the same relative relationship that either history or reasonable extrapolation indicates?

4. Do participant actions result in resolution of the problem? Can that resolution be either better or worse than the state of nature?

5. Do experienced participants believe the scenario and the outcomes?

IV. THE VARIETY OF EMERGENCY MANAGEMENT EXERCISE ALTERNATIVES

A Historical Comparison of Exercise Alternatives

The first chapter of this study discussed in general the current standard Federal Emergency Management Agency model of exercise types. The five exercise structure has developed over the past forty years to meet needs for a progressive exercise program for training and testing. However, it is by no means the only solution to the characterization of exercise types.

Morentz provided a chronology of early exercise systems that offers a useful perspective on the development of exercise types. In 1965 the Office of Civil Defense identified three categories of exercises, shown in Table 5, aligned for contrast with the current Federal Emergency Management Agency model.

The Seminar Exercise identified in this classification was essentially a Tabletop Exercise, with extensive verbal discussion by the participants of problems and the identification of appropriate actions and decisions. Seminars included the option to use simulation techniques. Operational Exercises resulted in the activation of the emergency operations center and, in some cases, the actual movement of field resources. Morentz pointed out that this type of exercise could be used for individual training and for training the entire system.

Table 5.
1965 Office of Civil Defense Exercise Model

1965 Model	FEMA Model
....	Orientation Exercise
....	Drill
Seminars	Tabletop Exercise
Operational Exercise	Functional Exercise
....	Full Scale Exercise
Test or Evaluation Exercise	....

Source: James W. Morentz (1984), <u>Exercises: A Research Review</u>, Rockville, MD, Research Alternatives, 30.

The category of Test and Evaluation Exercise was distinguished from the Seminar and the Operational Exercise by the addition of specific performance grading criteria (Morentz 1984a, 29-30). Morentz argued this was not actually a separate exercise type, as either Seminars or Operational Exercises could be used for evaluation. However, I believe the identification of evaluation is significant, as this establishes evaluation as a separate exercise goal.

In 1974 the University of West Virginia published an

exercise handbook for local jurisdictions with a six level exercise program, as shown in Table 6 (Morentz 1984a, 30-31). This categorization is important as it provided a progressive exercise program. Of particular interest is the use of two formats that are of potential value as simple command center staff training tools, the Seminar Exercise and the Map Exercise.

Table 6.
1974 University of West Virginia Model

1974 Model	FEMA Model
....	Orientation Exercise
Seminar Exercise or Feasibility Exercise	....
Command Post Exercise	Functional Exercise
Map Exercise	Tabletop Exercise
Emergency Operations Simulation Exercise	Orientation Exercise
RADEF Exercise	Functional Exercise
Field Exercise	Full Scale Exercise

Source: James W. Morentz (1984), Exercises: A Research Review, Rockville, MD, Research Alternatives, 31.

35

The 1974 model introduced two other new types of exercises, one of which (the Radiological Defense, or RADEF, Exercise) was intended to be computer generated. The Emergency Operations Simulation Exercise is described as "an orientation for key emergency officials only" (Morentz 1984c, 31). The Operational Exercise of 1965 was replaced by the Field Exercise.

In 1979 the Defense Civil Preparedness Agency published an exercise handbook for the Crisis Relocation Program, an attempt to deal with the effects of nuclear war by relocating populations out of high value target areas prior to the onset of conflict (Hilburn and Parker 1981, 5). This book referenced a five level exercise system as shown in Table 7 (Morentz 1984a, 32-33). This model adopted three exercise types designed to be played in a relatively informal format. The Orientation Exercise, as we now know it, made its appearance and was identified as the first step in the progressive sequence. The Discussion Exercise was formalized as a way to exercise group problem solving in a seminar environment. The Tabletop Exercise with formal message play was also introduced in this model; although there had previously been exercises of this type, this is the first use of the term.

In 1984 Morentz (1984b, 2-3) proposed a very similar exercise program. The significant differences from the 1979 model were in the last two exercise categories. The Operations Exercise was renamed the Emergency Coordination Simulation, but remained focused on functional issues in the emergency operations center. The Field Exercise was also renamed to become an Outside Disaster Drill.

During this same time period, there had been significant experimentation in how hospitals conduct disaster drills (a

Table 7.
1979 Crisis Relocation Exercise System

1979 Model	FEMA Model
Orientation Exercise	Orientation Exercise
Discussion Exercise	....
....	Drill
Tabletop Exercise	Tabletop Exercise
Operations Exercise	Functional Exercise
Field Exercise	Full Scale Exercise

Source: James W. Morentz (1984), Exercises: A Research Review, Rockville, MD, Research Alternatives, 33.

subset of the overall community emergency preparedness program). Although five possible types of exercises have been identified, as shown in Table 8, the influence of the Joint Commission has effectively restricted most hospitals to conducting facility level Full Scale Exercises.

Seliger and Simoneau's (1986, 186) work is interesting as it identified common themes found in other sources, but from the different perspective of a small, compact entity. They identified the importance of complex exercises with unexpected

Table 8.
Hospital Disaster Drills

Simulation Board Game	similar in format to Dennis Kelley's Search and Rescue Simulator
Tabletop Drill	similar to a standard emergency management Tabletop Exercise
Paper Drill	a Functional Exercise using all standard procedures but with patients simulated by their paperwork
Subsystem Drill	a Functional Exercise
Mock Casualty Exercise	a Full Scale Exercise in the hospital

Source: Jerome S. Seliger and Joan Kelley Simoneau (1986), Emergency Preparedness: Disaster Planning for Health Facilities, Rockville, MD, Aspen Publications, 186-191.

events when they described the Simulation Board Game, one of the issues this study addresses with the simulation tools proposal. Also of interest is the Functional Exercise conducted with paper patients. This had some characteristics in common with the proposed In-Basket alternative that will be discussed in some depth in a following section (187).

In 1988 the United States Environmental Protection Agency (5) identified three basic exercise types, the Tabletop, Functional, and Field Exercises. The first of these, the Tabletop Exercise, was used to train participants in plans or procedures. The Environmental Protection Agency's characterization of this exercise type is important, because it introduces significant flexibility into the design of the exercise in three specific areas not previously addressed:

1.   Tabletop Exercises may range from informal discussions of emergency management issues in a general situation to a structured verbal analysis of the situation and step-by-step recital of the steps to be taken in a specific event.

2.   The number of functions exercised in a Tabletop Exercises may vary--one function, several functions, or all functions may be addressed.

3.   The depth to which any particular functional area is exercised may vary in Tabletop Exercises.

It is reasonable to suggest that, if the format of the Tabletop Exercise can be modified within fairly wide parameters, alternative exercise formats may have equal applicability.   The Environmental Protection Agency did recognize that a large number of exercises may fit within a given general classification, as shown in Table 9.

So far this discussion has focused on classification systems in use in the United States. Descriptions of other systems are not widely reported in the literature in the United States, but several exercise systems do exist which deserve attention. To meet existing international needs for training the

Table 9.
Environmental Protection Agency Exercise Classes

Tabletop Exercises:
...   Environmental Protection Agency (EPA) Tabletop Exercise
...   Federal Emergency Management Agency (FEMA) Tabletop Exercise
...   Chemical Manufacturers Association (CMA) Tabletop Exercise

Functional Exercises:
...   FEMA Functional Exercise
...   U. S. Coast Guard (USCG) On Scene Commander (OSC)/Regional Response Team Simulation
...   CMA Emergency Operations Simulation

Field Exercises:
...   EPA Full Field Exercise
...   FEMA Full Scale Exercise
...   USCG OSC/Local Response Team Exercise
...   CMA Drill and Field Exercises

Source: United States, Environmental Protection Agency (1988), Guide to Exercises in Chemical Emergency Preparedness Programs, Washington, DC, U. S. Environmental Protection Agency, 5-6.

Pan American Health Organization (PAHO) developed a Simulation Exercise as a single type of exercise. This approach implied that local facilities will be adequately prepared through the use of hospital drills. However, the drill format was not viewed as being particularly effective in preparing senior policy and administrative personnel. The PAHO model was specifically designed to address some of the same issues that the alternatives in this study address:

(1)   The relatively high stress and uncertainty under which staff must operate.

(2)   The need for critical assessment of information, much of which may be unreliable.

(3)   The importance of rapid decision making.

(4)   The need for coordination between agencies and technical services that do not normally work together (Wasserman 1983, 44).

Of this list, two issues, critical assessment and rapid decision making, are addressed in the Tactical Decision Game format. However, the PAHO exercise went beyond limiting the amount of information available for decision making. This exercise introduced a large amount of contradictory data to force decision makers to take a broader view of problems.

None of the alternative formats in this study addresses stress in the same way the PAHO process did. Exercise participants were not fully informed on exercise objectives and mechanics and were rapidly flooded with large amounts of information through messages. At the same time physical factors were addressed by varying the lighting, allowing the room temperature to rise, and not providing food or drinks (Wasserman 1983, 45). The PAHO format was a 7 hour exercise, allowing the stress techniques to have maximum

41

effects; the challenge is to find mechanisms that will produce similar effects in shorter events.

In 1993 Bob Overy, Leeds City Council Emergency Planning Officer, described a British Paper Exercise design. He categorized exercises as being Paper Exercises if they do not:

1.   Use an actual reconstruction of an incident with persons playing the role of victims.

2.   Require actual mobilization of facilities and equipment. Although Overy does not say so, by implication this includes the mobilization of field response personnel.

3.   Use actual buildings and communications (184).

Overy distinguished between two types of Paper Exercises, Liaison Exercises and Team Building Exercises, on the basis of the role that the exercise controllers play (183). In the Liaison Exercise the exercise control team was located in the same room as the participants and provided verbal or paper messages to facilitate exercise play. Each participating agency addressed its responsibilities in the scenario separately and liaised with the other agencies as needed. The exercise objective was to rehearse coordination procedures and to familiarize participants with the roles of each agency (185). This concept of separate problem resolution and coordination of the actions needed to carry out the solution is unique and may have real application when dealing with larger agencies.

In the Team Building Exercise, the exercise control team was located in a separate room from the participants and all inputs were provided by telephone or written message. This allows greater flexibility in play options and   evaluation.

42

Participants may be allowed to contact their agencies to order resources or to determine technical answers to problems. The detailed message flow generates a paper trail of exercises responses allowing a formal evaluation if desired (186).

The discussion of options for exercise systems is by no means static. As recently as 1996, Panaction Response International, an emergency management consulting firm, described four exercise types. The Orientation Exercise did not appear in their list. However, the Panaction Response Drill was equivalent to the Drill and the Limited Exercise to the Functional Exercise. Both systems included the Tabletop Exercise and the Full Scale Exercise (Panaction 1996).

Given the variety of formats described it is reasonable to assert that exercise types will not, and should not, remain static. Although the description of each exercise has necessarily been brief, and there are subtle differences in each exercise category, in general the evolution of exercises has developed consistent models that try to do the same types of things. Of interest is the relative small spread of exercise types designed specifically to meet the objectives of this study, the training of command center staffs in settings that do not require full operation of the emergency operations center. Reasons for this are not obvious, but may lie in the assumption that a progression from Orientation through Full Scale Exercises does meet all needs.

Role of Exercises in Emergency Management

The Federal Emergency Management Agency's standard model of emergency management processes is the cycle of mitigation, preparedness, response, and recovery. Briefly summarized, mitigation activities are those which seek to prevent a disaster from occurring or to reduce its effects should

43

it happen. Preparedness actions include training, planning, exercises, and equipping response organizations. Response actions are taken immediately prior to disaster onset, through the impact of the disaster, to the start of recovery. Recovery actions start after direct disaster effects cease, with the object of restoring normalcy (US FEMA EMI 1989c, 1-6-1-9).

In this model, exercises normally are seen as being a part of the preparedness phase of the cycle, whether for training, testing, development, or research. All of these activities fit under the description of preparedness activities as including:

> planning to ensure the most effective, efficient response, efforts to minimize damages, such as forecasting and warning systems, and laying the groundwork for response operations, such as stockpiling supplies and surveying facilities ... (US FEMA EMI 1990, II-2).

However, it is worth considering whether exercises actually can extend across all four phases of the cycle. Three alternatives present themselves as being worthy of consideration.

Discussion Exercises would seem to be well suited to assist in the development of mitigation strategy. The Discussion Exercise format would seem to easily facilitate group analysis of hazards, identification of suitable types of mitigation, and the setting of mitigation priorities. Used in this way, the exercise scenario becomes the focus of discussion. The mechanics of the exercise facilitate the interaction of the players in developing an effective consensus plan of action.

A range of exercises, from Discussion through Tabletop to an as yet undeveloped rigid simulation, offers options for use

44

in the response phase. Short exercises allow rapid testing of incident action plans for feasibility prior to their implementation. If a regular daily planning cycle (Perry 1987, 342) is used to prepare the incident action plan, exercise testing can be added as a step of that cycle. During the later stages of the response phase, exercises could test locations for recovery facilities and plans for the transition from response to recovery operations. The advantage of using an exercise format, rather than a brainstorming session or other decision assistance, lies in the relative rigor the use of a scenario, events during the exercise process, and after action review give the process.

Because the recovery phase varies significantly with the intensity of the disaster, the need for exercising may also vary. However, in complex, long term recovery efforts, state level policy and resource allocation questions come to the fore as Federal efforts are terminated. These would appear to be susceptible to improvement by the use of discussion based exercises as part of the problem solving process.

Exercises currently play an important role in the preparedness phase of emergency management. Preparedness for many agencies is the most visible and sustained portion of the emergency management program. If the role of exercises is expanded to other phases, the importance of alternate exercise formats to meet a variety of specialized needs may increase.

A Survey of Exercise Types

There are a wide variety of types of exercises that are potentially suitable for command center training. Table 10 shows these in approximate order of complexity.

45

Table 10.
Command Center Exercise Types in Relative Order of
Complexity (from least complex to most complex)

Type	Source
Orientation	emergency management
Discussion	emergency management
Skull Session	fire service
Decision Game	military
In-Basket	business
Drill	emergency management
Postal	gaming
Tabletop	emergency management
Role Play	business
Internet	emergency management
Paper	hospital
Functional (Command Center Simulation)	emergency management
Map	military
Command Post	military
Full Scale	emergency management

Note: Assessment of complexity is the author's, based on the complexity of problems presented to the participants, difficulty of exercise design and construction, and level of effort required to conduct the exercise. The assessment of complexity of Internet Exercises is based on WEBEX 98 and WEBEX II, both chat based exercises.

From a training or evaluation standpoint, exercise

complexity reflects three dimensions, the complexity of the mechanics of exercise design and management, the degree to which the mechanism of play simulates actual procedures, and the difficulty of the problem presented to the players. When developing a progressive program, all three must be considered in the exercise design effort. As exercises become more complex in design, play, and situation, they consume greater effort to develop and greater resources to play. However, only two of these dimensions, the mechanism of play and the difficulty of the problem are of importance to the participants. As the complexity of play, including such factors as number and depth of the messages, use of actual communications, and use of actual facilities, increases, the difficulty of the exercise increases. Similarly, as the difficulty of the situation increases, so does that of the exercise. An exercise that increases one dimension offers a moderate increase in difficulty; increases in both dimensions create a much greater difficulty. This relationship is shown in Table 11.

Table 11.
Increases in Exercise Difficulty

DIFFICULTY OF SITUATION	COMPLEXITY OF PLAY	
	Low	High
High	Moderate	High
Low	Low	Moderate

Therefore, exercise and training planners have several options for providing progression in training. First, by selecting exercises in the order shown in Table 10, progressive training will be offered. Second, within each exercise type there may be ways to increase the degree to which play approaches reality, with an attendant increase in difficulty. Finally, the complexity of the situation presented in the exercise scenario may be increased, with more information, more problems, greater interrelationship between the problems, and shorter time periods for problem resolution.

Exercise Alternatives Studied

Discussion Exercises

Discussion Exercises are a major category of exercise events. Structurally, the Discussion Exercise uses a scenario and a list of questions to generate participant discussions of the problem and the appropriate actions to resolve it. The Discussion Exercise provides role, responsibility, and operational environment familiarization for emergency management personnel.

This is the first level of exercise at which problem solving skills are employed. However, in general, Discussion Exercises do not fully exercise individual abilities to make real time, tactical decisions during actual operations. Tactical, in the emergency services context, can be defined as "directing activities toward specific objectives" (National Fire Protection Association 1990, 76). This implies the selection of a specific means of performing an emergency task along with the allocation of resources and time for problem resolution.

When actual operations are rare enough to not offer reasonable frequency of opportunities for training, careful design of exercises can provide many of the same decision points. Three exercises types, Discussion Seminars (as a specific type of event within the broader category), Tactical Decision Games, and What-If Games, provide acceptable tools to meet this need.

Discussion Seminars.

Morentz (1984c, 10-15) described the Discussion Seminar as the second step in a progressive exercise program, following the Orientation Exercise. It differs from the Orientation in purpose, to study planning and resource allocation, and in structure, with the introduction of problem solving activities.

A Discussion Seminar is based on a brief written scenario which presents the players a description of an emergency situation, including the locality, impact of the disaster, and the available resources. Questions accompany the scenario to explore roles, responsibilities, procedures, and capabilities. The exercise is normally conducted by the participants discussing the problems posed by the questions and reaching a consensus on the best approach for their resolution. Development of a variety of alternative courses of action is encouraged, and participants should record and follow-up on alternatives as part of a regular program of readiness improvement. The exercise is intended as a low or no stress instrument that can be used in a classroom, conference room, meeting area, or similar facility.

Evaluation. Discussion Seminars are simple tools that can be employed by facilitators with minimum training (Table 12 shows contents of an Instruction Sheet that could be provided to allow even a very inexperienced controller to manage this process). They are very low cost in terms of

49

production expenses (typically the cost of copying the scenario, questions, and facilitators guide), staff preparation time (usually less than one person day), and time to play. As such, the Discussion Seminar is a logical first step in a series of progressively more demanding exercises designed to take inexperienced personnel to a reasonable level of preparedness.

Table 12.
Exercise Instructions in a Discussion Seminar

General Description
Objectives of the Exercise
How the Exercise is Used
Exercise Components
Participant Supplies
Time Required
Number of Personnel Required
Required Facilities
Procedures

Skull Sessions.

Each month the American Fire Journal publishes a Skull Session, a single page scenario combined with a situation sketch, designed to stimulate tactical thought. These are typically used by Fire Departments as the basis for discussion of how to manage a major incident. This discussion may be informal or be conducted in a classroom supported by a chalkboard or an overhead projector (Ackerman 1996).

The Skull Session format is much like that of Morentz's

50

Discussion Seminar. However, each Session provides all of the information needed, as well as the questions to be asked, in a magazine, rather than in a meeting. This format allows individuals to use the session as the basis for personal study of the issues involved. It is worth noting that the Federal Emergency Management Agency uses a virtually identical format for classroom exercises in the Emergency Operations Center--Incident Command System Interface Course and in the Introduction to Emergency Management Course (US FEMA EMI 1990, III-56-III-59).

Specific contents of a typical Skull Session include the following types of information and questions:

Conditions - the day of the week, temperature, other current weather, and forecast weather ("Skull Session" March 1995).

Situation - type of incident, extent, how the incident is detected, and how the response is initiated ("Skull Session" March 1990).

First Arriving Company Officer - what are the tactical priorities, where will resources be deployed, how to gain access to the problem, and what support is needed ("Skull Session" August 1989)?

Battalion Chief - what is the possible development of the incident, how much help is needed, and how will operations be coordinated ("Skull Session" April 1989)?

First-In Commanding Officer - in a multi-agency event who is in charge, where will the command post be

51

located, and which tasks are single agency and which are joint ("Skull Session" May 1995)?

Incident Commander - what are the assignments for arriving units, what tactics will be used in dangerous situations, how can more resources change the situation, and what is the impact of the approaching weather ("Skull Session" February 1995)?

Tactical Decision Games.

The format of the Discussion Exercise can be modified readily from one that encourages discussion of plans and procedures to one that focuses on choosing the correct response options. United States Marine Corps personnel have been using Tactical Decision Games as a training tool to improve decision making skills since 1990. Tactical Decision Games are short written scenarios to which participants react by developing a plan of action. The Game scenario presents players a short, and deliberately incomplete, description of the situation. Because the player does not have perfect information, he or she must make reasonable assumptions as the basis for response to the situation, much as has to be done on a regular basis in actual emergency operations.

Three elements distinguish the Tactical Decision Game from the Skull Session, the Discussion Seminar described by Morentz, or the Federal Emergency Management Agency's Tabletop Exercise models. First, the Tactical Decision Game is played within a strict time limit. Second, stress is easily introduced through the use of more difficult scenarios or more restrictive time limits. Finally, Tactical Decision Games require, as an end product, a completed operations order.

Players must complete their decision making and order writing within time limits of between 5 and 20 minutes after they complete reading the scenario. The time limit introduces stress by forcing the players to make decisions based on limited knowledge by a deadline. The time limit also places the players in a more realistic environment; emergencies, like combat, are what John Schmitt (1994, 4) called "time competitive." Rapid action is essential to react to, contain, and ameliorate the threat the situation poses. The Tactical Decision Game places the player in the position of having to make decisions under realistic constraints.

The Tactical Decision Game asks for a specific product, the completed operations order. In both the Marine Corps and the Army, the five paragraph operations order is the single standard way to provide direction to tactical units. See, for example, John F. Antal's three interactive exercise books, Armor Attacks: The Tank Platoon (1991), Infantry Combat: The Rifle Platoon (1995), and Combat Team: The Captain's War (1998), for good examples of the use of the operations order as a method of controlling tactical operations. These are also excellent examples of very complex solitaire self-directed exercises. Because of the difficulty of constructing such interactive, text thread based exercises, this technique is not addressed in this volume.

Specifying this order format provides practice in developing the standard output of the military decision process. Because in small units the operations order is normally given verbally, the exercise provides practice in a basic communications skill, providing structured instructions in an understandable format to people who will have to carry them out. In addition, the game process can specify that participants will produce overlays--a sketch map of the situation area with

53

unit locations, areas of responsibility, and movement annotated. This forces players to translate broad generalities into finite actions that can be evaluated by the other exercise participants (Schmitt 1994, 3-5).

While the written operations order format is foreign to civilian emergency management, a similar order structure is already in place in the Incident Command System as used in wildland fire fighting. Known as the Incident Action Plan, it provides strategy for the next operational period (Carlson 1983, 217). The Virginia Office of Emergency Medical Services has developed a similar written Mission Order format to task its state level Emergency Medical Services Task Forces (COVA DH OEMS 1996b). And the emergency services in general are well used to verbal orders, ranging in complexity from dispatch instructions to complete oral incident action plans given on the scene.

Solitaire Tactical Decision Games. Tactical Decision Games can be used in two basic modes of play: Solitaire and Group. In the solitaire mode the player reads the scenario and determines the course of action to be followed. Solitaire Games exercise basic decision making and have the advantage of being short, usually requiring no more than 10 to 20 minutes. However, they lack the benefits of the interactive experience provided in the Group Game.

Group Tactical Decision Games: In the Group Games a number of players participate together. The most experienced player may be selected as a moderator to describe the scenario and control the game process. During the game the moderator also serves as a catalyst by introducing "what-if" options and questioning the reasons for decisions. After play the moderator leads the critique process in examining each player's solutions.

54

Schmitt cited several advantages to participation in group decision making exercises, including:

1.   The exercises can generate pressure, based on competition between the participants.

2.   Each participant receives rapid feedback on his or her ideas and problem solutions from the other participants.

3.   Requiring participants to issue orders gives them practical experience in working under a short deadline to perform actions they will have to perform in an actual event.

4.   Players broaden their understanding of decision making by listening to other participant's solutions.

5.   When participants are members of the same organization, they gain understanding of each other's thought processes, resulting in better team work during actual events.

Evaluation: The Tactical Decision Game appears to offer a uniquely focused tool to exercise decision making skills. Because the scenario is designed to only work decision issues, elements such as information gathering, technology employment, communications, and computer use are absent. As a result, players cannot divert their attention from decision tasks. Like the Discussion Seminar, Tactical Decision Games provide structured, low cost training that is easy to conduct.

What-If Exercises.

Playing "what if" is often regarded as an expedient way to frustrate forward movement in almost any type of management activity. By posing increasingly unlikely events preceded by the phrase "what if," the opponent of a course of action can eventually find one that renders a proposal inadequate. However, the what-if process is also potentially a powerful type of just-in-time Discussion Exercise.

Pagonis related examples of the use of this technique by the Allied Forces logistics staff during the Persian Gulf War to explore responses to possible scenarios. In the highly fluid environment, asking "what-if" questions associated with potential excursions from expected conditions allowed the staff to examine potential problems and potential solutions proactively. Among the advantages that he cited are that it:

1. Allows exploration of all possible problem areas in a plan, identifying the problems and potential solutions.

2. Reduces the degree of uncertainty associated with the developing situation.

3. Reinforces linkages among the various specialties involved in the operations.

4. Stimulates cooperation and collaboration in problem solving.

5. Encourages a more expansive view of potential courses of action (Pagonis and Cruikshank 1992, 101, 194).

As a result of use of this technique, Pagonis (104) "could honestly say that there was nothing that surprised us, and nothing that we weren't prepared for."

Evaluation. The What-If Exercise seems uniquely

suited to just-in-time exercising during all stages of an on-going event. Questions, such as "what if the hurricane accelerates and comes ashore six hours earlier than we expect now," have the potential to assist in identifying a wide range of impacts and resulting courses of action.

In-Basket Exercises

The In-Basket Exercise may be of particular value in the training of command center staffs in their essential duty of resolving support problems. An In-Basket Exercise is a type of simulation which requires the participant to use managerial skills to analyze, prioritize, and take action on items presented as the contents of an office in-basket. In-Basket Exercises have long been favored tools in assessment centers as they provide a way to determine the thought processes of candidates for employment or promotion (Tielsch and Whisenand 1979, 26). In addition, MacCrimmon and Wehrung (1986, 80), in their discussion of risk taking among managers, reported the use of an In-Basket Exercise as a tool for research in decision making under uncertainty.

In an In-Basket Exercise, the participant is confronted with a stack of messages that must be sorted and resolved in a limited time period. Typically the problems range from those of critical importance to meaningless distractors. The time available to deal with all of the problems does not permit in-depth contemplation of each, and no assistance is available. The participant takes action by noting on each problem instructions for its disposition.

The conditions for this exercise typically include the following:

1.   The exercise must be completed in a limited amount of time (typically one to two hours).

2.   The player is alone--no one can be reached for advice, instructions, or clarification.

3.   Action is taken based only on the information in the basket and in introductory instructions that set the scenario-- even if information is supplied it typically is incomplete, contradictory, or of minimal value.

4.   Solutions to problems are generated as instructions to the player's staff. These can only be short notes (Eitington 1989, 212).

The meat of the exercise lies in the scenario and problems that are presented. Tielsch and Whisenand (1979, 196) suggest that typical scenario instructions should include:

1.   A description of the role the participant is to play, including name and job title.

2.   Time limits, including a plausible reason for those limits.

3.   Directions that the player must decide on appropriate actions for all items within the exercise time line.

4.   Instructions that written action must be taken on each item in the basket. Options available to the player typically include to:

... specify actions for a staff member to take on an item that needs immediate action.

58

... identify what added information is needed and where it is to be requested from.

... delegate the action to another.

... group together for action those items that may be related, and

... inform others of the situation and the action taken.

Evaluation.

The In-Basket Exercise is very attractive as a training tool. Because of the way the exercise is designed, it can achieve high content validity by requiring players to do work closely related to their own duties (Tielsch and Whisenand 1979, 26). In addition, this exercise type is very flexible and can easily be used outside of normal training hours as a self-study aid. An acceptable model is the Risk In-Basket Booklet developed by MacCrimmon for research purposes--it provided four problems to be completed in 45 minutes (MacCrimmon and Wehrung 1986, 307-312).

The In-Basket appears to be especially appropriate for training command center staffs because it simulates the situation that may be encountered at a shift change. Typically key information will be conveyed in a general briefing, followed by a short face-to-face discussion with the off-going staff member. The new duty officer will be left with a number of unresolved or partly completed actions that must be sorted into priority order. Although primarily used for assessment and research, the In-Basket has the potential to provide excellent

59

training in problem recognition, placing items in order of priority, quick decision making, and clear written communications with other command center staff members.

Floortop Exercises

Another class of exercise, defined more by the tools used than by specific rules or goals, has evolved over the past two decades into common use. For lack of a better term, I have called this category Floortop Exercises because they are readily carried out in a large, clear floor area. However, the term Floortop is somewhat a misnomer in that they also can be conducted on sandtables, tabletops, magnetic boards, and even using specially constructed model cities, as well as on the floor. The key element is the use of miniature representations of the situation and the responding resources for enhanced realism, improved visualization of the situation, and increased participant involvement.

Formal literature in emergency management has largely ignored this category of exercise. However, there are numerous examples of such exercises in common use.

Sandtable Exercises.

The Army has long used this technique, and commonly refers to it as a Sandtable Exercise. The equipment used for the Sandtable Exercise varies in its sophistication--at the high end is a large box mounted on sawhorses and filled with sand that can be shaped into a representation of the terrain. However, a similar result can be achieved by simply scraping terrain markers in the dirt of a training area. This inexpensive training aid allows participants to easily group around the working area so all can learn from discussions and questions (Collins 1978,

107).

<u>Tabletop Simulators</u>:

According to Bahme (1978, 82-83), as early as the 1970s, the Virginia Fire Service Training Department used three dimensional structures and miniature vehicles, railroad cars, and aircraft on a table covered with heavy paper on which streets were drawn. This system incorporated an audio system to provide exercise radio transmissions.

In 1986 Furey (1986, 24) reported on the use of a large tabletop simulation at the Rockland County, New York, Fire Training Center. This device was developed over a period of 24 years by George Proper to provide fire officers a three dimensional panoramic view of major incidents for training. The tabletop represented a complete community with buildings, streets, industrial facilities, and rural areas. Emergency vehicles were simulated by die-cast models. Furey noted that participants rapidly accepted the models, became involved in the training, and were able to more easily visualize tactical problems.

This exercise technique has been used extensively. Probably the most widely known example was first reported by Cashman (1993, 17-19). Division Chief Donald E. Abbott of the Warren Township, Indiana, Fire Department constructed a three section simulation table which could be used to exercise 139 hazardous materials and emergency scenarios. This facility provided 234 buildings, 160 vehicles, and miniature response personnel. Abbott's exercise has become a staple of community emergency response training. In a typical case, the City of Greensboro and Guilford County contracted with Command Emergency Response Training, Inc. to conduct a two

61

day series of exercises on March 12 and March 13, 1999. Exercise events included Orientation Exercises on both days and a series of an ambulance-railroad accident, a Year 2000 response, a building collapse, and an in-flight collision between two aircraft with one aircraft falling onto a school (Greensboro-Guilford County Emergency Management 2000).

Floortop Exercises.

The British Transport Police use a room size floor plan model of a railroad line and surrounding suburban terrain to simulate railroad accidents. This elaborate simulator includes detailed scenery with buildings and equipment to scale ("County News: Cornwall" Autumn 1994, 15).

Rather less sophisticated is the approach suggested for Mass Casualty Incident Management training by the Virginia Office of Emergency Medical Services. Terrain features, roads, rail lines, and the accident site may be laid out on the floor with masking tape. Standard size colored file cards are used for emergency vehicles and to mark key exercise events. Patient conditions are written on file cards with triage decisions marked on the back. Because this exercise is intended to train a large number of students, players are assigned to duties in the same numbers as would be appropriate in the real event (COVA DH OEMS 1996c).

A slight modification has been made to this approach in floortop simulations conducted in the University of Richmond's Introduction to Emergency Services Management Course. For simplicity in assembling the exercise area in a variety of classrooms, the terrain, including roads, is marked on the floor with masking tape. Individual buildings are represented by laminated cards that can be marked on to represent the degree of damage. Miniature die-cast vehicles are used to represent the response forces, and golf tees the emergency agency personnel. This allows a larger area to be used than is the case with either the tabletop simulators or the fully assembled models. At the same time a reasonable degree of realism is retained.

Magnetic Board Exercises.

Linkoping University Hospital (1993) has developed a vertical board simulation system that uses magnetic symbols to lay out a complete simulated disaster. Responders, victims, the terrain, and vehicles are all represented by magnetic symbols and signs. The system uses representation of clock faces and magnetic hands to show the time of the accident and the current time. Also, a set of six magnetic simulated gauges are used to show weather conditions.

The MASCAP Mass Casualty Planner manufactured by The Command Post is a magnetic horizontal or vertical board simulator designed to be used in training and to control operations during actual incidents. This system of movable magnetic situation displays, scenario cards, management worksheets, and patient injury cards graphically represents the disaster scene. As a result, participants in training scenarios can develop a mental picture of the actual disaster. The scenario cards can be used to introduce complications to force command decisions. Magnetic pointers on simulated clock faces show time, temperature, overall weather, wind direction, and wind velocity (The Command Post 1993, 3, 24-25).

Evaluation.

The Floortop Exercise model presents many of the advantages of a Functional or Full Scale Exercise with few of the costs. Many of the limitations of actual responses can be simulated, such as space to stage resources, limitations of access and egress from the scene, exposure of other facilities to the disaster's effects, etc. At the same time, participants are able to act in their standard tactical configuration, assigning people to specific jobs, and using a complete incident command system. Multiple agencies and disciplines can be represented, and, because participants are presented with a visible set of circumstances, normal response plans can be stepped through. Based on the author's experience in using several variants, participant reactions are uniformly favorable.

Postal and Internet Based Exercises

The difficulty of involving the entire organization in a disaster exercise is a significant problem for statewide volunteer organizations and some state agencies. Due to travel distances, time required, and facility needs, getting participation from all levels may be difficult and expensive. To address this challenge, an exercise method must be able to be used simultaneously by all system elements with no requirement for travel to specialized training areas. Postal and Internet based exercises may offer a solution.

Postal Exercises have not been described in the emergency management literature, although there is a long tradition of playing chess and hobby wargames by mail. Postal Exercises are phased exercises with a limited, discrete problem presented by the exercise controller for player resolution in each phase. Participants solve the problem or take the actions called for in the phase instructions. After completion of one phase, players receive second, third, and successive sets of instructions until all exercise phases are played through. In each case, exercise phase results are reported by each participating unit to the exercise controllers. The level of play is less demanding than in other exercises, and the time schedule is longer. However, the primary difference from other exercise types is that organizations are players, vice individuals, and that the entire system can participate simultaneously.

The term Postal Exercise describes the exchange of taskings and results over some communications medium. Use of the mail is the method of choice for organizations with limited access to facsimile, radio, or on-line computer communications. Because postal play has been commonplace in chess and hobby wargames, the basic procedures are well tested and understood.

The Virginia Defense Force, a volunteer component of the Virginia National Guard, used a Postal Exercise (Exercise MAILBAG) to provide simultaneous training in basic command and control procedures for the entire organization. The format of the Postal Exercise was based on a detailed scenario mailed to each level of the organization, Brigade, Battalion, and Company, followed by exercise problems. The problems represented expected taskings that could be assigned to the units in a disaster, and each built on the information provided in the scenario and the preceding problem. Each problem required the participating units to submit reports using the same format that would be used operationally (COVA DMA VADF 1994, COVA DMA VADF 1995). The number of problems that can be worked in this format is limited; in the two MAILBAG exercises, three problems were used, with one problem a month on successive months to conform to monthly meeting schedules. However, the Postal Exercise offers an inexpensive way to exercise an entire statewide organization, both in terms of financial costs and human resources.

In 1995 and 1996 two successive annual hurricane exercises conducted by the Department of Emergency Services of the Commonwealth of Virginia were essentially Postal Exercises based on the use of facsimile transmission of situation information to state agencies. The initial two weeks of play for each exercise consisted of weather message traffic and daily situation reports. The Virginia Office of Emergency Medical Services, as Health and Medical Function manager for Virginia, used this information as the basis for internal exercises. At the end of each day, key staff members met to evaluate the messages and determine the actions they would have taken in an actual situation.

In March 1996 the members of the Local Emergency Planning Committee Internet Mailing List conducted a tabletop format exercise on-line. The exercise included the normal general situation description and exercise messages, to which participants reacted by providing their suggested actions. These suggestions were summarized by the exercise controller and provided back to the participants. Essentially the format replicated the standard Tabletop Exercise, given the application of Internet communications. This was the first use of the Internet for a complete exercise with which I am familiar. In general this exercise was a success, although it identified a number of areas for procedural improvements (Pasquarelli 1996).

On November 5, 1998 the Emergency Information Infrastructure Partnership and the Virtual Fire and Rescue Exposition hosted WEBEX, an Internet exercise based on the use of five chat rooms. This event assigned separate rooms to the Incident Command Post, Emergency Operations Center, Staging, Triage, and Media Briefing functions, and used designated communications officers to pass information from one function to another. With 77 participants, this was a large exercise (Sebring 1999, 17-18). In spite of general enthusiasm on the part of the participants, the medium of chat rooms does appear to have limitations, including difficulties in exercise control, the cumbersome nature of the communications process, and the inability of participants to easily track actions in progress.

Evaluation.

The two MAILBAG exercises conducted by the Virginia Defense Force provided an effective test of the Postal Exercise concept. In each exercise all 47 local units were provided a written scenario and detailed instructions on exercise play in the familiar format of the military five paragraph operations order. The instructions included directions on how to complete the reporting forms, which were standard communications templates already in use in the organization. Each exercise problem was designed as an exercise phase, with each phase building on the scenario and the previous phases. One month was allocated for play of each of the three phases of the exercise, to coincide with the regular monthly meeting schedule.

Participation was actually quite high for response to mail instruments in volunteer organizations. MAILBAG 94 resulted in a 27 percent return (25 of 91 possible phase problems). MAILBAG 96 showed a significant increase with a 66 percent return (61 of 93 phase problems). The higher return for the second exercise can be attributed to three factors: increased familiarity with the exercise format, increased familiarity with the communications formats being used, and the simultaneous introduction of other operationally oriented training.

67

The experiences of the 1998 and 1999 WEBEXs have not been formally evaluated as the basis for assessment of the effectiveness of Internet exercises. In both cases participants expressed feelings of great satisfaction with the exercise process in the immediate informal debriefings. Sebring (1999, 18) stated that "the experience is highly true to life." However, the presence of players not familiar in some cases with the role they were portraying and with only limited familiarity with the jurisdiction in which they were performing their duties makes it difficult to extrapolate to the value of the tool for a team not suffering from those disadvantages. In addition, the mechanism of communication, chat, requires familiarity and established procedures if communications are not to break down.

Inclusion of Postal and Internet Exercises as training tools seems warranted. These formats offer significant opportunities for focused training in functions that require the passing of information, direction, and reports up and down an organizational chain of command. This is a low cost option, as it does not require travel or significant time away from normal duties by participants. It may allow a larger number of persons or agencies to take part, especially if the agencies use the exercise messages as the basis for internal exercises. Because a clear paper trail is generated by each action (although for chat based approaches this does require an archive function), after action reviews are simplified. These formats may also offer greater flexibility for future technological growth.

Use of Simulation Tools

The exercise models described above are all predictable in their play sequences. Even if dynamic inputs are presented by controllers in response to player decisions, the essential thrust of the exercise is prescripted and predictable within the normal thought processes of the exercise designer. Exercise designers develop a Master Sequence of Events List to program the order in which events occur (US FEMA EMI 1989a, 60), essentially rendering the exercise static in its conception and control. As a result exercises are the products of the designers, not necessarily realistic depictions of a range of chance events.

Actual disasters are not so predictable. Earthquakes and tornadoes are notoriously difficult to predict in location, intensity, and timing. Even with large storms such as hurricanes, predictions of the course of the storm and its effects are subject to significant error down to as little as 12 hours prior to landfall (University Corporation for Atmospheric Research 1999). Therefore, it seems logical that it would be desirable to introduce an element of uncertainty to disaster exercises.

In 1979 Dennis Kelley (8) proposed the use of a simulation system to train search and rescue operations leaders in the various skills required for effective management of searches for missing persons. Kelley's simulator was built around a structured sequence of events with the introduction of chance at key points through die rolls. One or two dies suffice to give the exercise controller a wide variety of options in differing elements as shown in Table 13.

The use of dice to control exercise events is not uncommon, with its primary current use being in wargames produced for the hobby market. Although these board games are designed for hobbyists, the educated nature of the market makes provision of both a high degree of historical fidelity and a full range of operational considerations critical. However, this fidelity must be tempered with reasonable chance events that allow either side to emerge the victor. The mechanism adapted to make this occur is a combination of die rolls to provide the chance combined with detailed tables that interpret the outcome of chance. Such tables have been successfully used to simulate the results of combat and the limitations of terrain on operations (Dunnigan 1992, 19-20). They have even been used to reduce to the abstract such complicated relationships as national weapons production and strategic logistics interactions (Simonsen 1977, 80).

Table 13.
Kelley's Simulator Die Controlled Events

Selection of problem difficulty
Weather
Location
Time of day
Available resources
Resource turnover
Significant events leading to event resolution
Distracting events
Condition of victims

Source: Dennis E. Kelley (Fall 1979). "SAR Management Simulator." Search and Rescue Magazine, 9-13.

Evaluation.

I developed and tested a set of simulation rules for use in exercises to introduce elements of chance in scenario development. I used the architecture of Kelley's simulator as a basis for development and combined the use of die determined chance events with decision trees reduced to tabular form. The popularity of fantasy games has brought with it the availability of dies with a variety of numbers of sides and percentage dies. As a result it is possible to broaden the range of percentages that can be played to more accurately reflect local experience, historical data, forecasting, and other sources of scenario information.

The use of such simulation tools as essentially a rulebook for exercise operations appears valuable in two contexts. First, they allow rapid development and framing of key scenario elements, such as incident type and severity, month, day of the week, time of day, and weather conditions. As the number of events determined in this way increases, the potential number of variant scenarios increases geometrically. This ensures that scenarios do not become routine and predictable.

Second, they give exercise controllers a mechanism for introducing uncertainty into the actual play of the exercise. This uncertainty can effectively mirror the unpredictable elements that disaster response forces face when actually working to control disaster effects.

United States Army Exercises

Because of the nature of their responsibilities, all of the United States Armed Forces routinely participate in exercises, some of which are at the command center level and others full scale. One of the most comprehensive systems of exercises has been established by the United States Army. The Army defines thirteen standard types of training exercises; this schema is shown in Table 14 in the order from least to most complex, with their standard acronyms.

Table 14.
United States Army Exercise Types with Acronyms

Map Exercise	MAPEX
Drill	
Tactical Exercise Without Troops	TEWT
Fire Coordination Exercise	FCX
Command Post Exercise	CPX
Logistics Coordination Exercise	LCX
Situational Training Exercise	STX
Command Field Exercise	CFX
Lane Training	
Freeplay Maneuver	
Live Fire Exercise	LFX
Combat Training Center	

Source: United States, Department of the Army (1990), <u>Battle Focused Training</u>, FM 25-101, Washington, DC, U. S. Government Printing Office, C-2.

Of these, two, the MAPEX and CPX, are structured specifically to train command center personnel with no movement of field units. MAPEXs are designed to provide staff training in an organization's base facilities using limited communications. A CPX provides similar training with two significant additions - the staff is deployed with full equipment to a field location for a period of time, and the complete suite of normal operational communications systems are used. Thus the CPX includes elements of both a Functional and a Full Scale Exercise.

Map Exercises.

Map Exercises (MAPEX) are conducted as a low cost training option with minimum expenditure of resources, including staffing costs. MAPEXs are used to train operational unit staffs in teamwork, assessment, integration, and direction and control functions. Exercise play is driven by a scenario schedule of events. The resulting situation information may be depicted on area maps, terrain models, or sand tables. Communications are deliberately kept simple, using point-to-point telephone circuits (typically field telephones). A Map Exercise may be conducted in any available space, including either permanent or temporary facilities, such as tents.

Map Exercises require an exercise control structure. Controllers provide scenario information to the players in the form of reports from subordinate units, logistics data, intelligence, and mission results. In every case, the control staff is careful not to reveal information that would logically not be available to the participants. The size of this control team depends on the size of the participating organization and the complexity of the scenario (US DA 1984, 35-36).

It is important to understand that the concept of minimal expenditure of resources in a MAPEX is relative to the size of the organization conducting the exercise. For example, a sample Brigade level Map Exercise depicted in Field Manual 25-4 (39) required a separate control facility, six telephone lines, and an exercise control staff of 27 officers and noncommissioned officers.

Evaluation.

The use of Army exercise formats would appear to have

73

direct applicability to emergency management for several reasons. Army National Guard roles in disaster response are already large (US DA 1993, 1-5) and are expanding as the National Guard searches for mission alternatives (Daigle 1996, 16). In some cases (the State of Washington is an example), the Adjutant General of the National Guard has been given organizational responsibility for emergency management. Therefore, by adopting an Army model, commonality of terminology, procedures, and operations is encouraged between the military and civilian sectors. In addition, exercise procedures are clearly defined in Army Field Manuals (US DA 1990, US DA 1984), providing a baseline for exercise development.

However, the Map Exercise is fundamentally unsuited for emergency management use. The most basic objection is that this exercise model is designed for large organizations (with thousands of personnel) with a single mission focus and which can staff complete exercise control functions. The resources required to manage either exercise are far beyond local and many state capabilities. In many local jurisdictions emergency management offices have a single full time, part-time, or volunteer staff member. Similarly, at the state emergency management agency level typically a single employee is designated as the exercise training officer.

A review of Army documents indicates that Map Exercise supporting materials are designed for combat operations, not disaster response and recovery. This forces users to do a substantial amount of work to develop new materials to support simulation efforts. Finally, this exercise format requires extensive time to develop and play. As a result they are distinctly impractical for use on a regular basis by agencies with limited personnel resources and budgets.

Role Playing

Role playing is a common technique in management training. Julius Eitington (1989, 338) reported that two surveys of trainers uniformly gave role playing exercises very high scores on such factors as knowledge acquisition and retention, problem solving skills, and participant acceptance. The Federal Emergency Management Agency included a role playing exercise in its Introduction to Emergency Management course (US FEMA EMI 1990, IV-2-IV-9). Superficially, the role play would therefore seem to be well suited to use in training command center staffs.

However, there are significant drawbacks to this approach to training. It is difficult to role play with any degree of accuracy if you do not understand the role you are to portray. For example, asking an Administrative Assistant at a low level in a County Department to portray the role of an elected County Commissioner in a decision making exercise is flawed. The participant does not have to act within the same political constraints as the Commissioner and lacks the same frame of reference for policy matters.

Because senior policy level personnel within jurisdictions often do not play in exercises, their role has to be simulated by others. For example, in one recent Local Emergency Management Operations Exercise conducted in Virginia, the City Manager was the senior official present. The Mayor did participate, but only as a player in the simulated press conference, and not in a decision making role. Although studies have not been conducted to identify disconnects in the resulting decision making, it is likely that elected officials would not make all of the same decisions that their surrogate

75

role players make.

Role plays are excellent when the participants understand and have experienced the role--for example, everyone knows a difficult employee or customer on whom to model their behavior. However, the new emergency operations center staff member who has this as an additional duty and has never operated in an actual disaster does not have a reference model. As a result, they may have difficulty performing most emergency roles, with a significant decrease in exercise realism.

V. THE CONTEXT OF EXERCISES

To understand how these varied options can be applied as emergency management exercises, it is important to examine them using the same schema applied to other types of exercises and games. There are several possible approaches to the development of a scheme for the classification of exercises. For the purposes of this study, I have examined two possible taxonomies, termed the functional and the structural taxonomies. These two approaches describe what an exercise is from significantly different perspectives, contributing to our understanding of exercise design and use.

A Functional Taxonomy of Exercises

There is little reason to conduct an exercise unless that exercise meets specific needs of the agency doing the work and those of the individual participants. Experience and anecdotal reports indicate that exercises are often held because an agency has to meet regulatory or funding requirements. For example, the Joint Commission on the Accreditation of Healthcare Organizations requires hospitals to exercise on a regular schedule, and the allocation of Federal Emergency Management Agency Emergency Management Assistance funding was tied to completion of exercises. These requirements may create pressure to hold an exercise without having thought through what types of work the exercise is supposed to examine and what functions it is supposed to perform.

The most basic way of classifying an exercise is by the function that the exercise performs. The broad classes of needs of agencies and individuals create a functional taxonomy of what an exercise is designed to do, including the following purposes: training, testing and validation, system development, and research.

In 1989 the Federal Emergency Management Agency's Exercise Design Course defined an exercise as:

> An activity designed to promote emergency preparedness; test or evaluate emergency operations, policies, plans, procedures, or facilities; train personnel in emergency management duties; and demonstrate operational capability. (US FEMA EMI 1989b, 6)

The same source lists six ways in which exercises improve operational readiness:

> ... reveal planning weaknesses,
> ... reveal resource gaps,
> ... improve coordination,
> ... clarify roles and responsibilities,
> ... improve individual performance, and
> ... gain public recognition for the emergency
> management program (5).

Of these, three, improving coordination, clarifying roles and responsibilities, and improving individual performance are clearly training related. They are also virtually identical to three of the outcomes Morentz cites for training exercises.

Exercises for Training

Exercises are commonly accepted as training tools, for individuals in duties only performed during the exercise, for teams (such as the staff of an emergency operations center), and for complete systems. Hausrath (1971, 18) defined training as one of the three basic purposes for conducting an exercise. He identified three areas in which the requirements of the military profession are unique. These same characteristics apply in large measure to emergency response, and I have recast Hausrath's reasoning in a disaster preparedness context.

First, emergency response is fundamentally dangerous work, both personally for responders and for the members of the public the responder is trying to assist. The penalty for ineffective operations may be increased property loss, and it is not unusual that it will be increased incidence of serious injury or death. Even if everything is done correctly, there are still significant hazards and risk involved. This places a premium on safe training for the high risk situation--exercises offer a way to make errors, that otherwise might prove costly, in a no or low risk environment.

Second, disaster preparedness requires skills the emergency responder may rarely use, even in a career. Disasters are extreme events that are relatively rare in their onset. While many of the same skills are applicable to lesser emergencies, the normal day-to-day event does not severely tax the individual or the system in the same way as the disaster. Exercises provide a way to train vicariously for the extremes that will only be encountered in the true disaster.

Third, disaster response training is conducted in periods when there are no on-going disasters. The knowledge imparted in the classroom is largely built from the experience of others. It is historically based and tends to lag developments that shape the characteristics of future events. For example, hurricanes are increasing, not in frequency or power but in destruction due to

79

demographic changes that put more people and property in vulnerable areas. Flooding is becoming more destructive because of increased construction increasing runoff. These trends can be expected to continue. However, there is often general surprise when new events are far more destructive than even recent history would indicate should be expected. Exercises can be used to extrapolate what responders will face based on trends and reasonable futures.

Morentz (1984c, 7) stressed the value of Orientation Exercises, Discussion Seminars, and Tabletop Exercises as training exercises. He noted six outcomes for such events.

> ... clarifying plans and responsibilities,
> ... practicing resource management,
> ... improving coordination,
> ... clarifying interagency roles and responsibilities,
> ... improving individual performance and knowledge, and
> ... building confidence of emergency professionals (1-2).

While not all of these outcomes are specific training outcomes, they all contribute to training goals, and further confirm the close relationship between all of the potential functions exercises perform.

Exercises for Testing and Validation

Exercises are potentially low cost and high payoff ways to test or validate existing or new plans and procedures for emergency operations. As noted above, testing falls within the basic reasons to hold an exercise advanced by Morentz and the

Federal Emergency Management Agency. Hausrath (1971, 27) also embraced testing as a key exercise function and noted that wargames were used in that role in both World Wars. This extended to the use of ongoing games as a mechanism to test plans for operations in progress.

Daines focused on the use of exercises primarily to test a jurisdiction's emergency operations plan. At each level from the Tabletop through Full Scale Exercise, Daines (1991, 186-187) stressed the exercise as an evaluation tool. This view is consistent with the approach that defines separate roles and locations for training (the classroom) and testing (the sole reason to exercise). In actuality, the line between training and testing is a fuzzy one. Both functions can be accomplished in the same exercise model. It therefore appears cost effective to include elements in an exercise to do both functions.

The problem with using exercises to evaluate plans and procedures is that anecdotal evidence strongly suggests that inexperienced staff will simply do what they believe to be right without reference to the plan. Typically plans will be available, even at the specific work station, but will not be referenced by the participants. This is true even if the plan design includes quick reference checklists. For example, field observations of players in three Virginia Local Emergency Management Operations Exercises and a state level Medical Tabletop Exercise showed only isolated reference to available plans.

This suggests exercise design must be structured to force players to go step-by-step through the plan or procedure to be evaluated. The Discussion Seminar appears to offer some promise in this area, if questions are structured to elicit plan usage. Similarly, Postal Exercises can be structured to require use of specific procedures for reporting or directing action.

81

<u>Exercises for System</u>
<u>Development</u>

None of the emergency management sources consulted in the study identified initial system development as an exercise function. The operating assumption is that exercises should only be conducted when there is a plan in place, people have been trained, and the supporting infrastructure is operational. However, the experience of the Virginia Office of Emergency Medical Services suggests that exercises can perform a critical role in development of an integrated system of resources, plans and procedures, and command and control.

The experience in Virginia's health and medical Tabletop Exercises MEDEX 95 and MEDEX 96 has been that exercises can perform a wide variety of system development roles. In two of the most important the exercise serves as a time compressed Delphi technique for:

1. Identifying hazards, vulnerabilities, and the extent and impact of their effects. A normal hazards analysis process theoretically should perform this function. However, an exercise allows the sponsoring agency to use the participants as a consultative body to help identify excursions or overlooked dimensions.

2. Determining the consensus of emergency managers and responders on the best strategy and tactics for a particular incident type. In the Virginia case, the exercise brought together players who already had established plans and doctrine for specific incidents. By conducting the exercise, the sponsoring agency was able to develop a synthesis that could be incorporated in a workable state level response plan.

Exercises for Research

Exercises, especially those which result in quantifiable results, provide a framework for analyzing emergency management actions that is both relatively low cost and convenient. Actual disasters are messy from a research perspective--you have to wait for them to occur, control for a wide variety of extraneous variables, and perhaps not even have the needed data recorded in the heat of the event. In exercises, the researcher can control design and data collection to ensure that research needs are met.

Hausrath (1971, 132) pointed out that such analytical exercises are essentially controlled experiments. In such an exercise, the design ensures activity to be tested occurs when and how it would normally be expected to occur. Therefore, measurement and research tools can be in place to record quantitative or qualitative data on operational performance. This requires in most cases that research exercises be relatively rigid (see following section, A Structural Taxonomy of Exercises) and, for quantitative analysis, that results can be subjected to mathematical analysis. As a result, research exercises require additional time for design, data collection, and analysis.

Although exercise use for research is common in the armed forces, this use is rare in emergency management. I found no reports of specific research resulting from exercises in the literature, much less of exercises being designed for research purposes. Tactical Decision Games, In-Basket Exercises, and Floortop Exercises would seem to be appropriate vehicles for the study of command center decision making. Tactical Decision Games simulate the situation surrounding strategic and tactical decisions in an emergency, i.e.,

83

compressed time lines, incomplete information, and the need to format decisions in a way that facilitates communications. In-Basket Exercises have been used to research executive decision making and would seem to be useful in evaluating how priorities for action are set. And Floortop Exercises can be designed to generate quantifiable data about specific techniques, decision processes, and flow and resource control.

A Structural Taxonomy of Exercises

In addition to classifying exercises by their function, it is also possible to describe them by their internal mechanics. By using relatively broad criteria, emergency management exercises can be subjected to the same analysis used in other disciplines. Four distinct parameter sets can be used to describe command center, and indeed all, exercises. This categorization provides a framework for understanding specific exercise types, for developing alternatives, and for matching them against the needs of the using agencies. Summarized, the categories are:

1. By the rules used.

2. By the degree of situation knowledge allowed participants.

3. By the mechanism of play. (Hausrath 1971, 123-126)

4. By whether or not there is an opponent.

Alfred H. Hausrath identified the first three of the four category groups above. Hausrath's work is significant in that it defined characteristics of exercises that apply across the spectrum of possible methods of their construction. As a central figure for many years in governmental operations research and gaming, his insights carry particular weight based solely on his experience. However, they also clearly provided a theoretical foundation for exercise taxonomy that is lacking in other literature.

I also considered a fourth category in this study because it is central to exercise design and play mechanics. Whether or not there is an opponent may seem an unusual question for exercises not involving military operations against hostile forces. However, the mechanics of exercise design and play are heavily dependent on whether or not there are forces in the exercise not controlled by the players--a consideration that appears uniquely applicable to disasters.

Exercise Rules

The design of exercise rules has evolved into two distinct approaches to managing the process and results assessment of an exercise. Each offers significant advantages, and each has significant limitations. A review of existing models of emergency management command center exercise designs show that neither approach to rules is truly being applied.

Rigid Games.

Rigid games are distinguished by the use of detailed rules to govern the procedures of conducting the exercise. These define exercise phases or turns, the performance of organizations and units, and the results of specific actions. Changes in the situation, movement and logistics support of personnel, and results of actions are governed either by specific algorithms or by chance, using random number tables, die rolls, cards, coin tosses, or a spinner wheel. The exercise is played to a time schedule, which may be phase driven or be in some relationship to real time. The role of exercise controllers becomes to ensure that the exercise progresses according to schedule and in keeping with the rules.

Exercises conducted using a rigid game approach have several advantages. The exercise can be used to produce quantifiable results. A number of plays should provide a reasonable expectation of what the range of those results would be in an actual event. This may offer a reasonable degree of confidence for the development or modification of plans and procedures. This also means that for research and analytical purposes the rigid game appears to be superior (Hausrath 1971, 123-124). At the same time, because the results are not influenced by player position or reputation and because the rulebook removes the need for expert decision, this format may be seen as more impartial when used for training.

However, rigid games do require the development of a well thought out set of rules. Because these rules tend to be extensive, players and controllers must be trained in them if exercises are going to be conducted with reasonable dispatch. Poorly developed rules are a potential source of controversy and may detract significantly from possible learning by the participants. Therefore they require a disciplined development process based on research, careful construction, and testing, overall a significant level of effort (Dunnigan 1992, 127-132).

Free Games.

Free games are designed to be conducted without a detailed rule book. In its place, a competent and experienced exercise controller applies judgment to interpret situations and determine the results of participant actions. Such free games allow the controller to take shortcuts to maintain the pace of play, provide for less rigid mechanics of play, allow more factors to be used in assessing results, and require less detailed record keeping. However, the quality of the exercise is highly dependent on controller training, subject matter expertise, and operational and exercise experience (Hausrath 1971, 124).

Although Hausrath did not mention it, a case can also be made that free games also require a higher than normal level of participant experience, if the full value of the exercise is to be realized. Inexperienced personnel can easily draw the wrong lessons from a free game, especially if the exercise only addresses parts of the emergency response system. This is particularly true when technical systems have a high potential impact, with the effect of communications outages on the ability to control operations being an excellent example.

Analysis.

Historically, emergency management exercises have always approximated free games. None of the exercise systems I have studied has used a rigid game method, with the exception of Kelley's Search and Rescue Simulator. An examination of current emergency management exercise design and evaluation materials shows no mention of exercise rules in the sense of a rigid game rulebook.

The closest approximation to such a rulebook that readers may be familiar with is the rulebooks that accompany commercial hobby wargames. For an excellent description of how such rules are developed, see Wargames Design: The History, Production and Use of Conflict Simulation Games (The Staff of Strategy and Tactics Magazine 1977).

87

Whether emergency management exercises have even been free games is open to question, as little, if any, assessment of adequacy or impact of actions is normally undertaken during play. However, the use of an exercise controller to maintain the course of play seems to meet minimal requirements for a free game, even if this individual does not use a minimal rule set. Emergency management exercises would seem to be on the most unregulated end of the rigid to free continuum.

This reliance on free games may have valid, pragmatic reasons, although these are not widely stated. Rigid exercises, although in many ways simpler to conduct, do require training in how to apply the rules. Comfort in using a rulebook comes from multiple exposures, requiring that exercise controller staff be dedicated to that role. This is a time and personnel luxury many jurisdictions would not be able to afford. The reservations in terms of cost and time that Herman (1982, 16) reported about planning apply equally to exercises.

Rigid game rules also require common agreement on the effects of action and reaction. A broad sense of disaster effects has been described in such publications as the Federal Emergency Management Agency's Risks and Hazards: A State by State Guide (1990) and Principal Threats Facing And Local Emergency Management Coordinators (1991). Approaches to emergency planning emphasize the need for identifying the risk of disasters in the community (Foster 1980, 43-90; Herman 1982, 13-18; US FEMA EMI 1990, 2.3-2.5). Risk in emergency management is conventionally defined by the mathematical formula: risk = probability of event times impact.

However, nowhere is there similar broad agreement as to the effects of response actions. We understand individual

88

component interactions within the overall framework of their daily application in routine emergencies. For example, the fire service has a clear understanding of the dynamics of fire suppression as a chain of events (Davis 1985, 219-227). However, when we posit the disaster situation with multiple events involving multiple disciplines, the interactions are not defined nor well understood even at basic levels. This makes it difficult to create rules that are realistic and accurate at anything beyond the intuitive level.

A final objection to rigid rules may well be politically driven. A rigid game implies that someone can loose. To have senior officials not perform well against rigorous, defined criteria is fraught with negative political consequences at the local level. A free game offers much greater opportunity to speak of lessons learned and things to improve rather than specific event outcomes.

The alternative exercises proposed in this study are free games, although two introduce more rigid criteria. The Tactical Decision Game, with its emphasis on a final written order in a specific time period, has rigid features, although the order is not formally evaluated. And the introduction of Simulation Tools is a first step toward a more rigid framework by quantifying many of the scenario and timing decisions in the game.

Degree of Situation Knowledge
Allowed Participants

Hausrath (1971, 124-125) proposed two classifications of games, open or closed, based on the degree of participant knowledge. In an emergency scenario, there are many possible items of information important to successful resolution of the problems the disaster causes. They may include:

89

... available response agencies,

... the location of the response units,

... what their staffing level is,

... what their logistics status is,

... what percentage of an assignment is complete,

... the severity of the disaster,

... the area covered by disaster effects and related impacts, and

... whether immediate disaster effects are ongoing or have been completed.

Open Exercises.

If an exercise is designed as an open exercise, the participants will have full knowledge of the situation, the effects of the event, the actions of participating agencies, and the decisions of all players. This results in an exercise in which all participants may be in the same room with a single situation display. Open exercises considerably simplify some elements of exercise design and play, as, in effect, there is no need for information gathering processes.

Although Hausrath characterizes the open exercise as providing full knowledge of the situation, I believe this is too wide a description of the relationship of the players to the environment. Full knowledge implies the participants not only see but also recognize what they are seeing. The complexity of the situation may well preclude such knowledge, even in the early stages of a fairly simple exercise. This is particularly true of exercises set in unfamiliar locations, leading to the often observed behavior of fixation on available maps.

Participants often spend a significant portion of the early

part of an exercise studying maps to determine locations, spatial relationships, distances, and the effects described in the scenario. While not quantified in this study, my experience has been that this occurs in every exercise in which participants are using generic exercise problems. In its extreme form, participants develop hypothetical maps they can relate to if the exercise scenario does not provide a map. Observed behaviors in two Local Emergency Management Operations Exercises already described were the opposite of this. Personnel familiar with their locality rarely referred to, or posted information on, maps.

Closed Exercises.

In a closed exercise, situation knowledge is partially denied to the participants. Each player is aware only of the information that can be determined from his or her observation, radio traffic, reports from subordinates, etc. Results of actions are only available when they are reported by simulated field units to the participants. Hausrath (1971, 125) pointed out that this exercise type more closely approximates actual operations. The closed exercise is more realistic and more complicated for participants, and information flow becomes a critical component of play. Closed exercises are also significantly higher in stress.

From an exercise designer's view, the closed exercise is measurably more work to develop and conduct. Because exercise inputs differ based on the participant to whom they are directed, more inputs must be prepared for a given problem, and their content must be carefully designed to preserve the appropriate degree of partial knowledge. More exercise controllers are required to direct the flow of exercise events. And evaluation becomes much more complex, requiring careful

91

tracking of events to determine who knew what information at what time during the exercise.

Analysis.

Most exercises at the simpler end of the emergency management exercise spectrum are conducted as open exercises. The exercises examined in this study are no different. The presumption is that, for group learning by command center staffs at the introductory end of the exercise spectrum, the participants must operate from reasonably equal knowledge of the current situation.

However, this does not exclude the use of closed exercise techniques to develop teamwork and information sharing behaviors or to evaluate information flow. This can be simply achieved by controlling the routing of information so that, from the first, decisions must be made by the players as to who will know what and when. This may be as simple as selectively handing incoming messages to specific players, rather than giving everyone a copy. A more complex solution is to use telephone calls or a message center to deliver messages.

The routing of messages to a message center is the technique most commonly used in the Virginia Local Emergency Management Operations Exercises. Inputs come by telephone to the emergency operations center (EOC) message center. The message center operators must write down the messages and then ensure they are routed to the correct staff section within the EOC. As a result, in exercises observed in two jurisdictions, there was often wide disparity of knowledge of the situation in agencies in the EOC.

An alternative used to control situation knowledge in a

Roanoke, Virginia, airport disaster tabletop drill, on 3 December 1996, was to not allow responding agencies to enter the room in which the exercise was being conducted until they would normally have responded. As a result, these new players had only limited situation information when they entered play. This put a premium of use of information gathering techniques to rapidly gain the knowledge needed to perform their roles (Reed 1996).

Mechanism of Play

Hausrath (1971, 126-127) categorized exercises into two major classifications, hand-played and computer assisted. Hand-played games incorporated a wide variety of exercise methods. Therefore, for the purposes of this study it is useful to extend and subdivide Hausrath's classifications.

Hand-Played Games--Map Based.

In the general class of exercises characterized as played by hand (often also termed manual games), the earliest mechanism of play involved actually moving pieces representing military units on simulated terrain or on maps representing the operational area (Hausrath 1971, 5-7). This mechanism was retained for both land and naval wargames as a primary method of play into the 1950s (Perla 1990, photographs between 142-143). It is the basic method used for hobby wargames, even if those games have had the mechanics of play converted to computer support. The map based approach focuses on spatial relationships (time, speed, and distance) as a critical component of the exercise.

The advantage of the map based approach to exercises lies in enhanced realism and increased attention to the realities

93

of moving in an operational area. Spatial relationships can be easily analyzed by the participants. The difficulty is that a sophisticated playing area is often required with a large map designed to accommodate the unit representations chosen.

Hand-Played Games--Information Based.

In an information based, hand-played exercise maps may be present, but they are more in the character of adjuncts rather than the focus of play. The focus of play centers on information intake and processing, action based on the situation as it develops, and reporting of situation and needs. Rather than maps and spatial relationships, the heart of the exercise lies in written messages and problem solutions.

The advantage of information based exercises lies in their close approximation to the way that command centers actually operate. The key processes are the same as EOC processes. Specialized facilities in which to conduct the exercise are not needed. However, the disadvantage lies in the ease with which spatial and time relationships can be overlooked, with a corresponding loss of realism in play.

Computer Assisted Games.

Rigid games are uniquely suited for computerization of all of the functions of play, even including to some degree the decision making process. Military wargames now incorporate computer simulations at all levels from individual vehicle through theater and national level play (Perla 1990, 97-102 and Dunnigan 1992, 256-261). These simulations include the ability to realistically assess results and modify play accordingly in interactive near real time.

This trend has not generally extended to emergency management exercises, for four possible reasons. First, most emergency management exercises, as already noted, are very free games, with few functions suitable for automation. Second, development of computerized exercises is expensive in terms of software and hardware costs and personnel time. The latter is particularly important because the personnel needed to develop the exercises must have a high degree of computer expertise, exercise design expertise, detailed knowledge of disaster and response actions and their effects, and understanding of the full range of emergency management actions. These requirements exceed the human resources of almost any local jurisdiction and most states. At the same time, many emergency operations centers do not use computers as an essential portion of their operational equipment.

Finally, the lack of computerization may be tied to a lack of higher education on the part some emergency management personnel. While detailed demographics for emergency managers are not generally available, the lack of education can be inferred from the 1996 decision of the National Coordinating Council on Emergency Management to drop the requirement for a college degree for certification as a Certified Emergency Manager (CEM) ("CEM Degree Rule Reconsidered" 1996). The CEM credential is recognized as the national certification in the emergency management vocation. A past Chairman of the Accrediting Commission has suggested this decision was made because the college degree holding pool of potential applicants had been exhausted (Nellis 1996). Drabek's 1987 (81) study of emergency managers showed that less than half (31 of 67) had sufficient years of education to have completed a college degree. It is significant that Drabek's work (83) suggested this data may over-represent larger jurisdictions in the sample.

95

The discussion of use of computer support to emergency management exercises that has occurred has focused on computers in a truly support role. Robert McDaniel in a 1966 paper (60-61) highlighted the use of computer displays and computer maps as ways to make information available. He pointed out that existing hazard specific models can support the development of scenarios and that electronic mail systems can be used to store and analyze exercise messages.

Analysis.

Most emergency management command center exercises are structured as information based exercises. While this is the simplest approach in execution, it allows participants to make assumptions about the time and resources it takes to do things that are not justified. It would seem that the use of both map and information based exercises, or perhaps exercises combining elements of each, would offer the best mix of training and testing.

The alternatives for Discussion Exercises presented in this study are manual information based exercises. However, two options for map-based exercises are also presented. The Floortop format uses the classic map based game as the basis for the mechanics of play, complete with representation of terrain and individual vehicles. In addition, the Simulation Tools presented allow incorporation of rigid game features into a map- based exercise (although these can also be incorporated into an information based exercise as well).

This study has not addressed computer assistance to emergency management exercises because of my focus on simple alternative tools. In addition, once exercise play progresses to the use of the actual operational hardware and software, the exercise is no longer within the scope of this study. However, the computerization of emergency management functions using the Emergency Information System, EM 2000, or Softrisk does allow for automation of play by creating an event log, maintaining agency resource status, and providing a visual display for the exercise.

Presence of an Opponent

The involvement of an opponent in military wargames is central to how such games are played, both by the participants and by the control staffs. Opponents in this context may be thinking adversaries that react in a cogent manner to the strategies and tactics of the other side. This result typically is achieved by having an actual staff of players representing the adversary. Alternatively, in simulation models, the opposition may be algorithms or mathematical formulas that exact attrition based on enemy strengths. These devices ensure that the players do not have a free ride to their objectives, as a minimum, and that poor performance may actually lead to defeat.

From this we can conclude that scripting of an opposition in an exercise leads to incorporation of two important effects on outcome. These can be summarized as:

1.   Attrition - the reduction in available resources due to the effects of the adversary. Resources may be time, personnel and equipment, and supplies. At some point attrition may be severe enough as to preclude accomplishment of the player's objectives.

2.   Countervailing actions - actions of the opponent

97

actually block the actions of the player, leading to failure to accomplish objectives. At the outer limits of these effects, the player may actually be forced to concede ground, time, or other elements of value to the opposition.

Emergency managers do not tend to consider disasters as the enemy, except, possibly, at a visceral level. And, at least in my observation, it has been unusual that exercises result in a measurable defeat--in other words, the fire or the flood does not win. However, in the real world, the disaster occasionally does defeat the best efforts to effectively manage it. One only has to consider the vast devastation resulting from the breaking of levees in the Midwest floods of 1993 or from California wildfires to realize that even the best response may not be successful. The loss of vehicles, equipment, and response personnel lives in such incidents as the Texas City explosion of 1947 (Benson 1990, 89-96), the Chernobyl nuclear power plant accident (Illesh 1987, 6-10), or any of a series of urban fire events, highlights that the response forces do sustain losses. In the fifteen years from 1978 through 1993 annual fatalities in fire incidents ranged 21 to 64 paid firefighters and 44 to 99 volunteers (Washburn, LeBlanc, and Fahy July/August 1994, 61). Even at the most prosaic level, such concerns as the loss of mobility resulting from flat tires caused by disaster debris merit inclusion (Brooks 1995, 5).

Existing exercise models do not specifically include provisions for either attrition or countervailing actions. However, among the proposed alternative models in this study several options would appear to allow incorporation of these factors in exercise design.

At the simplest level, any exercise could be modified to include alternative courses of action that reflect a noncompliant disaster. For Discussion Exercises (and also for the standard Tabletop) this may be as simple as including scripted exercise questions on the line of:

> The river has continued to rise. As a result the team you have assigned to sandbag houses on Tailor's Lane is in danger of being cut off. What actions would you take?

When Simulation Tools are used to direct play, the inclusion of negative events is somewhat easier. However, such events may have to be structured based on the scenario as well as being made conditional on player actions. Thus at intervals set in the exercise instructions a die could be rolled to determine if certain sorts of events happen. As an example, a possible event might be a fire truck collision with a carload of evacuees trying to reach shelter. If fire trucks have not been dispatched, the exercise controller would not place this event in play.

VI. AN ALTERNATIVE EXERCISE COOKBOOK

To translate theory and practice into a useful manual that emergency managers can use to plan and conduct simple exercises, I constructed and tested a set of directions for the exercise models. The models selected were those that appeared, based on the literature and exercise theory, to most closely meet the criteria included in Table 4 and that offered reasonable expectations of medium to high exercise validity. In each case test exercises were conducted using as subjects students in two courses, Introduction to Emergency Services Management and Managing Emergency Operations, at the University of Richmond, members of the Commonwealth of Virginia's Health and Medical Emergency Response Team, and members of other voluntary disaster response groups.

In each case, exercise subjects had previous exercise experience in the full range from Tabletop Exercises to Full Scale Exercises, as well as experience in actual disaster events. Based on their critiques of the various exercise models, I refined procedures for each exercise and developed a standard method of describing directions for their use. Exercise development processes as taught in exercise design courses (US FEMA EMI 1989a) and as modeled in available exercise design software (Cliffside Software, Inc. 1998) are complex, with a large number of steps, and requiring a wide range of sequential development products. These also were simplified to provide a development flow within the capacity of a small emergency management staff. The resulting design, play, and critique procedures are included in an Appendix.

APPENDIX

AN ALTERNATIVE EXERCISE COOKBOOK:
Models for Exercises to Train Command Center Staffs

AN ALTERNATIVE EXERCISE COOKBOOK: Models for Exercises to Train Command Center Staffs

1. INTRODUCTION:

a. **Purpose:** This manual provides detailed instructions for the design, conduct, and evaluation of exercises for training emergency operations center staff personnel, for testing plans and procedures, and for research in emergency management.

b. **Objectives:** Exercises described in this manual are designed to supplement existing orientation, drill, tabletop, functional and full scale exercise models and provide increased flexibility in conducting a progressive exercise program.

c. **Scope:** This manual describes procedures for designing and conducting emergency operations center simulation exercises that do not require the mobilization and movement of response resources or the use of actual operational facilities and communications. It supplements standard procedures for the design and conduct of exercises as taught in the Federal Emergency Management Agency Emergency Management Institute's Exercise Design Course.

2. STANDARD EXERCISE ELEMENTS:

a. **Individual or group exercise:** Most exercises are structured for group activity, even if the group is physically widely dispersed. However, some exercise designs may allow solitaire play for individual training.

b. **Time:** Time used in exercises may be either actual time or exercise time. Exercise time is:

(1) **Scenario time:** Scenario time is exercise time that does not change in relation to the passage of actual time in the exercise. Scenario time changes in relation to specific events written in the Master Sequence of Events List. Changes in scenario time may be from minutes to days.

(2) **Phase time:** Phase time is scenario time based on the start of specific phases in a phased exercise.

(3) **Actual time:** Actual time is 24 hour clock time measured in local standard or daylight time.

(4) **Compressed time:** Compressed time is time based on a ratio of one actual hour of exercise play to a specific number of hours of simulated time. Typical compression ratios are one hour of actual to four or six hours of simulated time. Compressions of greater than 1:6 are not recommended unless only a limited number of issues are being considered in the exercise. In general compressed time works best for exercises that consider broad issues that are not time sensitive. For detailed tasks, compression will often end up with the task actually taking longer to do in reality (such as filling out a message) than is allocated for it in the exercise.

c. **Phasing:** Exercises may be designed either to use discrete phases or to flow without obvious breaks in time and play.

(1) Phases should be considered when

exercise objectives are sequential and would be accomplished at different times in an actual event, when the mechanism of play introduces breaks in the exercise process, or when the exercise scenario logically consists of separate events. The method best suited to incorporation of phases of play is the Postal Exercise. Discussion Seminars and Tactical Decision Games can incorporate phases by new scenario information and new problems for resolution after completion of a previous set. In-Basket Exercises can incorporate phases by providing a new in-basket for each operational period.

(2)   Exercises in which the scenario and problems flow in a continuous manner more closely represent a real emergency event. Any of the exercise formats in this manual may be conducted in a continuous manner, with the exception of Postal Exercises.

d.   **Standard exercise instructions:** The format for exercise instructions to players and controllers will vary based upon the type of exercise. However, the following basic elements should be considered for inclusion in any exercise:

(1)   **General Description:** This section provides a basic overview of the exercise level and type of emergency.

(2)   **Objectives:** The exercise objectives should be clearly stated as criteria that can be measured on completion of the event.

(3)   **How The Exercise Is Used:** This provides the basic exercise type and when it is to be used.

(4)   **Exercise Components:** List the actual

physical parts of the exercise, including documents, maps, forms, etc.

(5) **Participant Supplies:** List the supplies the exercise participants will need to supply.

(6) **Time Required:** Give the estimated time it will take to complete the exercise.

(7) **Number Of Personnel Required:** Give the minimum number of players or agencies that must participate in the exercise.

(8) **Required Facilities:** Describe the type of physical facilities needed to conduct the exercise.

(9) **Procedures:** Provide a detailed description of how the exercise is to be conducted.

e. **Output:** Exercises should result in two classes of end products. Both reflect participant solutions to problems posed in the exercise.

(1) **Oral solutions:** Participants may determine the correct solution to exercise problems by discussion and provide those solutions to exercise controllers orally. Oral solution is the least formal approach to exercise output. However, for it to result in lessons learned that can be tracked, oral solutions must be documented by the exercise controllers or participants at least in bullet statement form. Discussion Seminars are ideally suited for use of oral solutions, with key lessons learned summarized on a flip chart or in an after action questionnaire. Tactical Decision Games which specify an oral operations order or incident action plan use the

oral solution format.

(2) **Written solutions:** Written solutions require the participants to provide written orders, a written plan, messages, or other forms of documentation of the desired solutions. This more formal approach is better suited to testing plans and procedures and as the basis for research. All exercise types may require written outputs during or at the end of the exercise.

3. **EXERCISE PLANNING AND PREPARATION PROCEDURES:**

a. **Develop exercise objectives.** Objectives must be written, specify measurable end behaviors or outputs, and be focused on a specific training, testing, or research outcome. "To have an exercise" or "to train in emergency procedures" or "to meet certification requirements" are not acceptable objectives. "At the conclusion of the exercise players will be able to correctly prioritize incoming damage reports using the standard operating procedures" is measurable - they either do it or they don't. It is focused on damage reports. And there is a clearly desired outcome.

b. **Determine and invite the desired participants.** Exercise participants will depend on the objectives of the exercise. Where possible participants should always be those who will actually fill the emergency operations center duty positions being exercised during an actual event. Remember that you also need to train alternates and those that will staff the evening shift.

c. **Develop the primary scenario.** Some scenario details can be determined by use of the simulation tables in this manual. In building the scenario remember that the more complex the scenario is the more difficult it is for the participants, and the more experienced they must be if they are to profit from it. Plan to stretch, not to overwhelm, the players. As a minimum the scenario should identify the following:

(1)   The type of emergency to which the organization is reacting.

(2)   The month, day, time, and place of the event.   Month, day, and time may be determined using simulation tables as long as results are consistent with the type of emergency being simulated.   If the disaster event could happen on today's date and at today's time, the use of the actual date and time reduces the possibility of confusion.

(3)   The severity of effects. This should be developed using historical data for typical events experienced in the area of the exercise. Severity of ongoing conditions may be determined by use of simulation tables.

(4)   The tasked unit and its resources. Baseline resources may use actual unit strengths or be constructed for a simulated unit. Actual resources for use in exercise play may be determined by use of simulation tables.

d.   **Select the appropriate type of exercise.** Select based on desired exercise level, training objectives, available personnel and training time, and facilities.

e.   **Create a Master Sequence of Events List (MSEL).** The MSEL should specify what events will happen in what order and at what time during the exercise. The MSEL also identifies to whom the events happen or become known

107

and in what format the information will be presented. To simplify the exercise design process and to increase the value of the MSEL for controllers, it may be valuable to identify what actions the players are expected to take based on the event.

(1)   Discussion Seminars and Tactical Decision Games will not have a MSEL in the standard sense. The questions posed with the scenario in these two exercise formats essentially serve as both the MSEL and the exercise messages.

(2)   In the In-Basket Exercise the items in the In-Basket are the MSEL events and also serve as the exercise messages.

f.   **Develop and write the script for exercise messages for each event reflected on the MSEL.**

(1)   Messages may be written simulations of radio, telephone, or fax communications messages using the standard message format of the organization. If communications systems are used (as they are in enhancements to Floortop Exercises), the message may be an actual radio transmission. In Floortop Exercises some messages may be presented to participants visually, for example, as an increase in the area covered by flood waters by putting down additional flooding markers.

(2)   Messages should provide the following information:

(a)   The originator of the message.

(b)   To whom the message is directed

(either by name or by duty position).

(c)   A time of the occurrence or of the message transmission.

(d)   The actual information to be conveyed as a text.

(e)   For controller use, a specific message or event number to allow tracking by the MSEL.

g.   **Prepare adequate copies of all materials for use by participants and by controllers.** The number of participant copies and to whom these copies go may be used as a tool to increase exercise stress and to evaluate information flow. The fewer the number of copies distributed the higher the exercise stress and the greater the demand for information flow. In Discussion Seminars and Tactical Decision Games each participant will normally be given a copy of the materials. However, in Floortop Exercises distribution of information may be restricted to those who could see an event to force participants to use information dissemination procedures.

h.   **Obtain and set up adequate facilities for the exercise.** These facilities may be a conference room (Discussion Seminars, Tactical Decision Games, In-Basket Exercises, and Postal Exercises) or a training room with a large open floor space (Floortop Exercises). Break-out rooms may be used to form participant groups and to separate field response personnel and their command post from the staff of the emergency operations center. Use of actual command post or emergency operations center facilities is not required and may actually distract less experienced participants from focusing on the limited issues presented in the exercise.

i.   **Assign adequate staffing for the exercise functions.**

(1)   Exercise Controllers run the exercise by supervising delivery of exercise components and messages and ensuring play conforms to the MSEL. In general, all of the exercises described in this manual can be conducted by a single Exercise Controller. Floortop Exercises may require additional Controllers to supervise play in separate facilities or by specific agencies. Controllers should be chosen based on familiarity with both exercises in general and the specific roles and events of the exercise in question.

(2)   Exercise Observers are used to record participant actions in specific areas to assist in evaluation of plans and procedures or in the development of research data. Observers should be carefully briefed on the behaviors and outputs they are observing for and be provided appropriate worksheets to help in recording the data.

(3)   Exercise Evaluators are used to observe and critique generalized processes during the exercise. In most cases the evaluation role in the exercises described in this manual can be effectively handled by Controllers and by a thorough after action review by the participants.

4.   **WHAT-IF EXERCISES:**

a.   **Description:** What-If Exercises are exercises designed to clarify roles and response actions for a single point in an emergency situation through discussion of actions to be taken if a certain event happens. The What-If Exercise is unique in that it can be used both for training and for gaming specific response actions in an ongoing emergency. Although this seems to be a very simple exercise tool, it actually requires a high degree of sophistication to pinpoint problems that will benefit from this type of exercise.

b. **Level:** What-If Exercises address specific responses taken within the Emergency Operations Center. Participants represent their actual emergency duty assignment.

c. **How These Exercises Are Used:** What-If Exercises may be used for:

(1) Training personnel who will be assigned to any emergency operations center duty position.

(2) Determining the best course of action in an actual developing emergency.

d. **Exercise Components:** What-If Exercise components include:

(1) **Scenario:** A scenario is presented orally preceded typically by the words "what if?" The scenario is brief and focuses on a single change in an emergency situation. During actual events the scenario is provided by the ongoing event and the "what if" statement is followed by a possible change in the situation.

(2) **Discussion Question:** The discussion question is embedded in the scenario statement.

e. **Participant Supplies:** Participants may have access to copies of organization plans and standard procedures applicable to their normal duty assignments.

f.   **Time Required:**

(1)   **Exercise Set-up:** None required.

(2)   **Exercise Play:** From 2 minutes to 30 minutes, depending on the complexity of the problem, the number of participants, and in an actual event the time allowed by the situation.

g.   **Number Of Personnel Required:**   The individual posing the question serves as the Exercise Controller and moderates discussion. The What-If Exercise works best when based on small group participation with three to five players.

h.   **Required Facilities:** The What-If Exercise can be held anywhere.

i.   **Exercise Set-Up:** No exercise set-up is required.

j.   **Mechanics Of Play:**

(1)   **Group Activity:** What-If Exercises are small group or two person activities in which personnel are assigned to roles they would or could perform in an emergency.

(2)   **Time:** Time for the purposes of exercise play is scenario time or actual event time. Time does not normally change during the discussion.

(3)   **Phasing:** Specific phases are not required in the exercise.

(4)   **Sequence Of Events:**

112

(a)   The Exercise Controller asks the "what if" question.

(b)   Participants assume roles based on the duties they are performing at the time. For training exercises, individuals should assume the role they will normally be assigned to in a real event.

(c)   Participants discuss the question provided and determine roles, responsibilities, actions to be taken, equipment needed, communications requirements, or other factors they feel need to be resolved.

(5)   **Output:** The exercise will result in oral solutions to problems. Normally solutions are not captured, unless the exercise is being used specifically to prepare improved plans or procedures. The value of the exercise lies in the participants thinking through a problem and arriving at a solution.

k.   **Advantages:**

(1)   The What-If Exercise has no associated costs and requires no development effort. Questions are posed by the Exercise Controller based on his or her perception of needs and events.

(2)   Flexible exercise length allows delivery to be tailored to available time.

(3)   Participant involvement is high and discussion lively.

(4)   The exercise can be conducted any time that a low activity level permits. During an actual event a planning team can be assigned specifically to examine "what if" issues.

(5)   The exercise is very informal and low stress. In an actual event, the exercise may actually relieve some stress by developing solutions to potential problems.

l.   **Limitations:**

(1)   The informality of the exercise format may cause participants to not take the exercise seriously.

(2)   Lessons learned are not recorded. Although the participants will have prepared to deal with the situation, their learning is not captured for others.

(3)   Scenarios must be highly focused on one problem that can be resolved.

5.   DISCUSSION SEMINARS:

a.   **Description:** Discussion Seminars are exercises designed to identify roles, responsibilities, and operational methods for emergency responses through discussion of actions to be taken in response to a specific scenario. The Discussion Seminar differs from the standard Tabletop Exercise in that it focuses the scenario at one point in time, participants receive all the problems (messages in the Tabletop model) at the same time, and group problem solving is required.

b.   **Level:** Discussion Seminars may address operations within any size area. Participant organizations represented may be at any level from state agency to local agency.

   c. **How These Exercises Are Used:** Discussion Seminars may be used for:

   (1) Training personnel who will be assigned to any emergency operations center duty position.

   (2) Testing of allocations of roles and responsibilities in emergency plans against agency expectations.

   d. **Exercise Components:** Discussion Seminar components include:

   (1) **Scenario:** The scenario should provide a basic description of the emergency situation and a response tasking to the organization.

   (2) **Map:** If participants are not familiar with the operational area a map with sufficient detail to allow them to visualize the problem should be attached.

Example of a Discussion Seminar Scenario and Discussion Questions

This scenario is designed for an organization that does not have a permanent emergency operations center (EOC). The exercise objective is to identify how the EOC should be set up in the available facilities. The questions used are examples of the types of questions that might be used. Note that questions would be prepared for each participant in the exercise to address their particular responsibilities.

115

SCENARIO: Your boss sticks her head in your office and says "we have a disaster. Open up the EOC in the conference room. I'll have the other sections send staff representatives." When you ask what happened, her answer is "I don't know, but Janet will fill you in." When you ask how bad, how long, etc., the answer is "it's real bad. We'll be here a long time cleaning this one up." When you enter the conference room you see a long table with ten chairs around it. At one end of the room there is a white board mounted on the wall. There is a small table at the other end with a regular phone and a separate line with a conference phone head. You have the emergency operations plan in your hand. The one door is in the middle of the wall so that you enter midway on the table. The people you see in the room now came in just behind you. They are waiting with expectant looks on their faces as though they expect you to tell them what to do.

QUESTIONS: For the Emergency Manager:

1. How will you organize the EOC? What functions will be performed in this room, and to whom will you assign them?

2. To turn the conference room into a functioning center, what are the first five things you need to do?

3. What steps do you need to take to find out the status of the emergency?

For the Administrative Assistant: etc.

---

(3) **Discussion Questions:** Discussion questions should be provided for the organization as a whole and for key duty positions within the organization. Questions

may address responsibilities, plans and procedures that would be followed, organizational and individual equipment requirements, and safety and supervision issues. Depending on the time allocated for the exercise, questions may be broad to encourage group discussion or focused to elicit specific responses.

e. **Participant Supplies:** Participants should bring with them copies of organization plans and standard procedures applicable to their normal duty assignments.

f. **Time Required:**

(1) **Exercise Set-up:**

(a) Approximately 5 minutes to lay out exercise components for participants.

(b) Approximately 10 minutes to brief participants on exercise procedures and the problem.

(2) **Exercise Play:** From 30 minutes to two hours, depending on the complexity of the problem and the number of participants.

g. **Number Of Personnel Required:** One Exercise Controller will be required to distribute the problem, keep time, and refocus participants when needed. Participants will be as identified by the agency hosting the exercise. The Discussion Seminar works best when it is based on small group participation with three to five players. If more are involved, it may be useful to split the participants into several groups.

h. **Required Facilities:** The Discussion Seminar is

designed to be held in a conference or training room with seating either around a conference table or that can be positioned in a circle or half circle to facilitate discussion.

      i.   **Exercise Set-Up:** Exercise set-up for Discussion Seminars is minimal. Provide one copy of the exercise instructions, scenario, map, and problems for each participant, and place the copies at their seats. Position one additional seat out of the primary seating area for use by the Exercise Controller. Provide a clock so participants can easily see how much time remains.

      j.   **Mechanics Of Play:**

      (1)   **Group Activity:** Discussion Seminars are group activities in which personnel are assigned to roles they would or could perform in an emergency.

      (2)   **Time:** Time for the purposes of exercise play is scenario time. Time will not normally change during the discussion. However, a real time limit is set for the exercise and will be enforced by the Exercise Controller.

      (3)   **Phasing:** Specific phases are not required in the exercise.

      (4)   **Sequence Of Events:**

      (a)   Participants are briefed on the exercise instructions.

      (b)   Participants are assigned to roles based on their normal emergency duties. The exercise scenario will specify which roles must be filled.

(c) Participants read the exercise scenario and use the map as necessary to orient themselves.

(d) Participants discuss the problems provided and determine roles, responsibilities, actions to be taken, equipment needed, communications requirements, or other factors as specified. Where possible, leadership of the problem solution should rotate between all participants, with each directing the discussion of questions focused on their responsibilities.

(5) **Output:** The exercise will result in oral solutions to problems. The most effective way to capture these solutions is through a post-exercise questionnaire in which participants review the lessons learned and identify agendas for action. Example questions might be "what are the three most important actions you must take to improve your capability for response" or "what agency do you need to coordinate with that was not represented in the exercise?" An alternate method is to use flip charts to record comments during an after action review.

k. **Advantages:**

(1) The Discussion Seminar is very low cost in both materials and staff time to develop and conduct. One individual can easily develop the materials needed in an 8 to 16 hour period.

(2) Flexible exercise length allows delivery to be tailored to available time.

(3) Participant involvement is high. Often

participant commitment to change after the exercise will be high.

(4)   The use of a post-exercise questionnaire provides a road map for individual and group action and can be the basis for a transition into a more formal tasking for change.

l.   **Limitations:**

(1)   Follow-up on lessons learned requires management support and regular checking. There is a tendency for interest in corrective actions to decrease over time.

(2)   Tactical decision making can only be exercised in a limited way.

(3)   Scenarios must be relatively simple to allow their comprehension quickly. Complicated scenarios will delay and sidetrack discussion.

6.   TACTICAL DECISION GAMES:

a.   **Description:** Tactical Decision Games are discussion games that focus on the rapid assessment of a situation, even if only partial knowledge is present, and the determination of a specific plan of action. They differ from the standard Tabletop Exercise in the use of very limited time, the tight focus on one issue, and the introduction of stress.

b.   **Level:** Tactical Decision Games are tactical exercises designed to cover operations within any operational area. Participant organizations represented may run from state level agencies to local agencies.

c.   **How These Exercises Are Used:** Tactical Decision Games may be used for:

(1)   Training supervisory personnel in emergency decision making.

(2)   Research in emergency decision making styles and outcomes.

d.   **Exercise Components:** Tactical Decision Game components include:

(1)   **Scenario:** The scenario should provide a basic description of the emergency situation. Full knowledge of the emergency and its effects is not necessarily provided to the players. In writing the scenario, the longer the scenario is the more time participants will need to read and understand it and the more complicated their discussions will be. A long scenario will thus be more stressful in the limited time.

(2)   **Map:** Participants receive a map with critical known information and the current disposition of response resources.

(3)   **Problem:** Participants are tasked to produce a written or oral incident action plan for their immediate actions based on their mission, resources, and situation.

e.   **Participant Supplies:** Participants may use a standard form for the completion of the incident action plan if their agency uses one.

f.   **Time Required:**

(1)   **Exercise Set-Up:**

(a)   Approximately 5 minutes to lay out exercise components for players.

(b)   Approximately 10 minutes to brief participants on exercise procedures.

(c)   No set-up is required for solitaire play.

(2)   **Exercise Play:** From 5 minutes to 30 minutes, depending on the complexity of the problem, the level of staff discussion appropriate, and whether the incident action plan will be oral or written. Most Tactical Decision Games should be from 5 to 15 minutes in length.

g.   **Number Of Personnel Required:**

(1)   For group play, one Exercise Controller will be required to distribute the problem and enforce the exercise time limit. Participants will be as identified by the agency hosting the exercise.

(2)   For solitaire play, the individual participating in the exercise for personal skill development is the only player.

h.   **Required Facilities:** The Tactical Decision Game may be held anywhere that two or more participants can gather. This includes in a conference or training room, in normal office space, or in a command center. No particular facilities are required for solitaire play.

Example of a Tactical Decision Game Scenario and Problem

SCENARIO: You are the Chief of the Jonesboro Volunteer Fire Department. As you are reviewing a grant application to purchase new equipment, dispatch tones your station "Jonesboro Volunteer, respond Engine 12, Truck 12, and Chief to grade crossing accident on Long Mile Road at the CSX tracks. Freight train hit a school bus. Injuries reported and the train has derailed. Rescue 26, Medic 25, Medic 27 also responding. Time of 1347." Under state law, you will be the Incident Commander.

You arrive on scene, approximately half a mile down a dirt access road from the grade crossing (see the map below), to find two engines and the first ten cars of the freight train derailed. The county handicapped school bus is on its side, partially trapped under one of the engines. Although the accident is a mess, there is no fire and no obvious hazardous materials releases (and you have not seen any placards). Medic 27 is on scene blocking the road ahead of you. The driver tells you his paramedic is in the wreckage trying to determine how many kids there are on the school bus. You hear Medic 25 and Rescue 26 calling the ambulance on scene: "Medic 27, this is Medic 25 - I have Rescue 26 with me. How do we get to you? Jonesboro Fire has their trucks blocking the access road up here." As the driver from Medic 27 reaches for the microphone, you tell him to have Medic 25 and Rescue 26 hold position.

PROBLEM: Be ready to brief your incident action plan in five minutes. Be sure to address assignments, set up, and traffic flow.

i.   **Exercise Set-Up:** Exercise set up for Tactical Decision Games is minimal. Provide one copy of the exercise instructions, scenario, map, and problem for each participant, and place the copies at their seats. Position one additional seat out of the primary seating area for use by the Exercise Controller. Provide a clock so participants can easily see how much time remains.

j.   **Mechanics Of Play:**

(1)   **Individual Or Group Activity:** Tactical Decision Games may be group activities or used for solitaire play. If used as a group activity, one individual should be designated as the supervisor who will issue the incident action plan.

(2)   **Time:** Time for the purposes of exercise play is scenario time. Time will not change during discussion. However, a real time limit is set for the exercise and will be enforced by the Exercise Controller.

(3)   **Phasing:** Specific phases are not required in the exercise.

(4)   **Sequence Of Events:**

(a)   Participants are briefed on the exercise instructions.

(b)   A leader is appointed with responsibility for issuing the Incident Action Plan.

(c)   Participants read the exercise scenario and use the map as necessary to orient themselves.

124

(d)   After participants have read the scenario, the real time clock is started. Participants discuss the scenario and advise the leader on their perception of the best course of action.

(e)   The leader prepares and issues the Incident Action Plan.

(5)   **Output:** Participants will develop a completed Incident Action Plan in their agency's standard format directing the actions they feel appropriate to resolve the situation. The Incident Action Plan may be oral or written. If oral, an Exercise Controller should record the key details for use in the critique. All solitaire play should result in a written Incident Action Plan.

k.   **Advantages:**

(1)   Tactical Decision Games train participants in decision making under time constraints with imperfect knowledge of the situation. This effectively mirrors the conditions for front line tactical supervisors in emergency response.

(2)   These exercises can be used in a wide variety of training settings, including very informal ones.

(3)   The short time required for the exercise makes their use very low cost in terms of staff time.

(4)   The option for solitaire play allows these exercises to be used by individuals who wish to improve their decision making capabilities.

125

l.   **Limitations:**

(1)   The scenario must be carefully written to allow even the unimaginative to visualize the conditions they are confronted with.

(2)   There is no single best solution for most problems. Although this is true to life, it may frustrate some users of this exercise method.

(3)   Completion of the exercise using the ground rules of minimum time and a fixed output requires a high degree of participant discipline.

7.   **IN-BASKET EXERCISES:**

a.   **Description:** An In-Basket Exercise is an exercise conducted using the contents of a simulated in-basket of messages waiting action in an emergency operations center.

b.   **Level:** In-Basket Exercises are designed for use by emergency operations centers staffs at state and local jurisdiction levels.

c.   **How These Exercises Are Used:** In-Basket Exercises may be used for:

(1)   Training personnel who will be assigned to staff emergency operations centers in the correct procedures and priorities for handling messages, tasks, actions, and information.

(2)   Evaluating the appropriateness of emergency operations center standard operating procedures on

the prioritization of work.

       (3)   Research on staff internal decision making procedures and priorities.

       d.   **Exercise Components:** In-Basket exercise components include:

       (1)   **In-Basket:** A physical container will be provided to contain messages waiting for action. If an emergency operations center uses an electronic mail system or electronic tasking systems, these systems will be loaded with simulated emergency messages to function as the in-basket.

       (2)   **Scenario:** The scenario will provide basic information about the emergency situation and indicate that the messages in the in-basket are leftovers when the individual's predecessor in the position was relieved. Typically, no additional information will be available, and the individual who worked before the participant is unavailable to answer questions.

       (3)   **Messages:** Messages will be provided in all standard formats, and some non-standard ones, in use in the emergency operations center. Messages will include situation information and reports, taskings, requests for assistance, requests for reports, or other typical emergency information. Messages will vary in age from minutes to hours, or even days, old, and in priority from very low to very high. Some messages will be unrelated distractors.

       e.   **Participant Supplies:** Participants should bring with them all command and control supplies they would normally have available in an emergency response. This may

127

include:

(1)   Operational checklists and plans.

(2)   Standard reference materials.

(3)   All types of forms used in the emergency operations center.

f.   **Time Required:**

(1)   **Exercise set-up:**

(a)   Approximately 15 minutes to lay out supplies for the participant and set up the in-basket and the participant work station.

(b)   Approximately 10 minutes to brief participants on the exercise process.

(2)   **Exercise play:** Approximately one to two hours, depending on the number and complexity of the problems presented.

g.   **Number Of Personnel Required:** One exercise controller is required to start the exercise and to evaluate exercise play at its conclusion. The standard exercise format requires one participant. If an entire staff is exercised, the participants should be designated by the agency hosting the exercise.

h.   **Required Facilities:** The In-Basket Exercise should be conducted in an area that provides an adequate work area for the participant. If a computer based command and control system is being used to store the messages, the participant must be provided access to a terminal.

      i.   **Exercise Set-Up:** Exercise set-up for the In-Basket Exercise is minimal. Provide the in-basket with all messages and one copy of the scenario at the participant's work station. If a computer based command and control system is being used, set up the terminal for system access. If multiple participants are involved in the exercise provide each with a unique in-basket.

      j.   **Mechanics Of Play:**

      (1)   **Individual Or Group Activity:** In-Basket Exercise may be conducted for a single individual (the traditional use) or for the key staff of an emergency operations center. If the In-Basket Exercise is conducted for a staff, some problems included in any participant's basket should require coordination with other staff members, or even be actions that should be given to another for resolution.

      (2)   **Time:** Time for exercise play is real time.

      (3)   **Phasing:** Specific phases are not required in the exercise.

      (4)   **Sequence Of Events:**

      (a)   Participants are briefed on the exercise instructions.

      (b)   Participants read the exercise scenario to orient themselves.

129

(c)   Participants are provided their in-basket for action.

(d)   If the exercise is being conducted with a staff present, participants redirect messages or coordinate solutions one-on-one or in groups as appropriate.

(5)   **Output:** Each message in the in-basket, or its electronic counterpart, must be acted upon and specific directions provided for its disposition. This may be by:

(a)   Notation on the document to file it with no action.

(b)   A covering routing memo forwarding it to a more appropriate emergency operations center staff section for action.

(c)   A covering routing memo recommending action by a senior official.

(d)   A situation or other formatted report incorporating the message's information.

(e)   A completed request for assistance to another agency.

(f)   An outgoing radio or telephone message providing instructions.

k.   **Advantages:**

(1)   The In-Basket Exercise is low cost to

develop and conduct in both materials and staff time.

(2)   A wide variety of exercise problem messages provide realistic training in prioritization of effort.

(3)   The exercise format is ideally suited for training single individuals newly assigned to emergency operations center duties.

(4)   The format supports both evaluation of existing internal standard operating procedures for staff work and research in emergency operations center decision making.

l.   **Limitations:**

(1)   The exercise format may be seen as threatening in agencies that customarily use assessment centers for promotion testing.

(2)   Exercise messages must be carefully crafted to avoid swamping participants with too many highest priority items.

(3)   The exercise format, unless expanded to use a staff, lacks the elements of real time, oral coordination and social interaction found in other exercises.

8.   FLOORTOP EXERCISES:

a.   **Description:** A Floortop Exercise is an exercise conducted using representations of personnel, equipment, terrain, and cultural features on a large surface, typically a floor, table top, or sand table. The use of semi-realistic scenery and emergency response unit representations allow easy

131

visualization of relationships in the operation.

b.   **Level:** Floortop Exercises are tactical exercises designed to cover operations within a small area. Participant organizations represented include the range of emergency services and key supporting organizations within a jurisdiction.

c.   **How These Exercises Are Used:** Floortop Exercises may be used for:

(1)   Training of personnel who will be assigned to command post duties as supervisors at the Division, Group, Branch, Section or Command level in an incident command system.

(2)   Familiarization level training of emergency operations center staff with field emergency operations.

(3)   Training of emergency operations center staffs and field supervisors in emergency operations center and incident command system interface procedures.

(4)   Testing of interface procedures for agencies operating at the incident scene during an emergency.

(5)   Research on the interaction of supervisory personnel during operations at the incident scene during an emergency.

d.   **Exercise Components:**

(1)   **Minimum Requirements:** Exercise components depend on the complexity of the exercise.

However, as a minimum the following are required:

(a)   Masking tape to lay out roads, bridges, and railroads. Recommended width is half inch or one inch.

(b)   Colored construction paper to mark forest areas, water, and other natural and disaster features. Suggested color coding is:

Wooded areas	Green
Water (lake, river, stream, pond)	Blue
Flooding	Blue
Fire	Red
Hazard spills	Orange
Buildings (concrete, brick)	Grey
Buildings (wood)	White
Debris	Brown

(c)   Yarn to indicate boundaries, primary routes, communications circuits. Suggested color coding is:

Area of operational assignment	White
Primary route	Yellow

Alternate route	Green
Communications coverage	Red

(d) Markers for command posts and specific points. These can be cut from standard white or colored file card material. The recommended shape is a rectangular 3" by 5" file card with one end cut to a point. Cards can be laminated with spaces for identification of point TYPE and AGENCY.

(e) Simulated vehicles and personnel. Vehicles can be made by labeling standard rectangular 3" by 5" file cards with the vehicle type and identification. Cards may be color coded to indicate vehicle or agency type. Cards can be laminated with permanent identifications marked on them or with spaces for identification of AGENCY, UNIT NUMBER, and CREW with an audiovisual pen. Almost any type of small marker can be used for personnel--one recommended option is golf tees.

(f) An exercise clock. This may be a real time clock, a clock face you move the hands on to represent time elapsed, a chalk or white board on which you write the simulated time, or a fast time clock.

(g) Message forms and log sheets. Use the standard ones in use in your agency.

(2) **Controller Supplies:**

(a) Scenario description and master sequence of events list.

134

(b)   Simulation tables and dice.

(c)   Controller record sheets.

(3)   **Exercise Enhancements:** The following can be used to enhance the realism, and thus the training value, of the exercise.

(a)   Small sized vehicles, buildings, bridges, scenery, and figures. Die-cast vehicles sold under a wide variety of brand names are of an optimum size for full floor top simulations. Other scenery elements may use supplies intended for HO scale model railroads. Railroad tracks may be represented by HO scale model railroad track. Use of scenery elements should be planned to allow participants to move around the exercise area without damaging the scenery elements.

(b)   Exercise radio communications. Exercise communications can be simulated by use of inexpensive 49 MHz headset radios. Multiple channel units allow assignment of frequencies to the various command, tactical, and dispatch nets that would be used in a real event. Single channel units should be checked to ensure frequency compatibility with other units already in use.

(c)   Terrain features. Hills can be simulated with styrofoam sheeting in various thicknesses. These may be spray painted a neutral color (light green or light brown) to give a more natural color. Several layers of sheet can be used to build up taller features--to allow placement of units on the terrain slope, make successive layers narrower than the lower layer by at least a vehicle width.

135

e.   **Participant Supplies:**   Depending on the complexity of the exercise, participants can be expected to bring with them all command and control supplies they would normally carry with them in an emergency response. This may include:

(1)   Operational checklists and pre-plans.

(2)   Standard forms.

(3)   Clip boards and other administrative supplies normally carried.

(4)   Identification vests for duty positions.

f.   **Time Required:**

(1)   **Exercise set-up:**

(a)   Approximately 30 minutes to two hours to lay out exercise map and scenery.

(b)   Approximately 15 minutes to lay out supplies for participants and set up participant work stations.

(c)   Approximately 15 minutes to brief participants on the exercise process.

(2)   **Exercise play:** Approximately one to four hours, depending on the number of units represented, the area covered, and the complexity of the scenario.

g.   **Number Of Personnel Required:**

136

(1)   **Exercise controllers:** From one to four controllers are required to provide scenario inputs and control play, depending on the size of the exercise area, number of agencies participating, and the complexity of the scenario. For large area exercises with complex scenarios and individual agencies actually represented, it is desirable to have one controller for each agency. Exercise controllers also serve as exercise evaluators.

(2)   **Participants:**   Representatives of agencies with roles either in the incident command system or in emergency operations center positions.

h.   **Required Facilities:** Depending on the size of the area covered and the number of participants there are three options:

(1)   **Meeting Room Floor:** A large clear floor can be used to set up the exercise map - for a county or city level problem you will need at least a space 12 feet by 12 feet. The more complicated the area and the scenario, the more simulated units participating, and the more actual exercise participants, generally the more floor space required. Ensure that sufficient space is available to allow a margin around the exercise map for participants to move freely.

(2)   **Table Top:** A large table top, at least the size of two 3 foot by 6 foot folding tables placed side by side, can be used for the exercise map. This is an ideal size for a problem within a limited portion of a jurisdiction.

(3)   **Sand Table:** If a sand table or an outside sandy area is available, the exercise map and scenery

can be constructed on the sand. A sand table is a large box, filled with sand, allowing the easy modeling of terrain features.

i. **Exercise Set-Up:**

(1)   Develop a map of the operational area to be simulated. Include on the map all natural and cultural features that have a role in the exercise.

(2)   Develop a listing of all resources that will be available for play. Include in the list not only those of the jurisdiction's departments, but also those that would normally be available as mutual aid.

(3)   Using masking tape, scenery components, simulated terrain features, simulated buildings, etc. construct on the floor or table top a representation of the operational area.

(a)   When laying out roads, allow sufficient width to accommodate the size of model vehicles used. Suggested width of the road is 4-6 inches for two lane to 6-12 inches for four or more lanes.

(b)   For floor simulations, allow additional space around features so that participants can move around the operational area without damaging the scenery.

(4)   Position resources in the normal locations they would be positioned in the operational area. For example, place the normal complement of fire vehicles at a fire station.

(5)   Establish an area for resources that would

be available in the exercise but which are not located within the area represented. Label each resource and place the appropriate number and type of vehicles on the labeled area. A separate table should be allocated for this purpose.

(6)   Prepare an area in which resources sent out of the simulated area can be held. If, for example, a hospital is some distance away, have an area in which ambulances destined for that hospital can be placed until they would be available again.

(7)   If specific facilities not within the simulated area will play, prepare an operating area for their staffs. This includes use of a separate room for an emergency operations center or a dispatch center.

(8)   Test communications that will be used to ensure they are functional.

j.   **Mechanics Of Play:**

(1)   **Group Activity:** Floortop Exercises are group activities in which personnel are assigned to roles they would or could perform in an actual emergency.

(2)   **Time:** Times may be exercise time, compressed time, or real time. If real time is to be used, exercise controllers must determine before the start of the exercise the times that would be required for the variety of different actions that may occur during the exercise.

(3)   **Phasing:** Specific phases are not required in the exercise. Events should flow in the normal order that would be expected in the type of emergency being
139

simulated.

(4)   **Sequence Of Events:**

(a)   Participants are briefed and allowed to view the operational area.

(b)   Participants are taken out of the room and controllers make any modification necessary to represent the immediate onset of the emergency.

(c)   The first responding players are returned to the room. They may now take those actions they would normally take in the situation.

(d)   Resources are added and additional players admitted to the room only on request of the initial responders to the controllers, either directly or through a dispatch center.

(e)   Controllers determine the time required for and results of player actions.

(5)   **Output:** The exercise should result in a series of player actions that would result in containment of the emergency situation. This series of actions may be documented by radio logs or written messages.

k.   **Advantages:**

(1)   Participants feel the exercise is significantly more realistic than Discussion or Tabletop Exercises.

(2)   Participants are exposed to problems resulting from distance, time, and speed.

(3)   Participants have the opportunity to visualize spatial relationships on the emergency scene.

(4)   Each participant can be assigned a specific tactical role with resources to manage.

l.   **Limitations:**

(1)   Floortop Exercises require substantial space for the set up of the exercise area.

(2)   Floortop Exercises are relatively expensive in time required for exercise set up and in the actual cost of exercise scenery and response unit vehicles and markers.

(3)   This exercise format can only depict a limited operational area, making it useful only for emergency scene training or training in interactions between the scene and an emergency operations center.

(4)   The resolution of individual components of the emergency situation require either controller judgment or use of simulation tools.

9.   POSTAL EXERCISES:

a.   **Description:** A Postal Exercise is an exercise conducted by exchanging direction, information and simulated action by mail (hence the name), electronic mail, or fax.

b.   **Level:** Postal Exercises are tactical and staff

exercises designed to cover operations within any operational area. Participant organizations represented may include state agencies and local jurisdictions.

c.   **How These Exercises Are Used:**

(1)   Training of personnel who will be assigned to field command posts or emergency operations centers in specific resource tasking, situation reporting, and results reporting procedures.

(2)   Testing message procedures.

(3)   Research on effectiveness of tasking and reporting procedures.

d.   **Exercise Components:**

(1)   A standard scenario is included to describe the situation at the exercise start.

(2)   Exercise instructions provide specific, step by step instructions on how to complete the exercise.

(3)   Exercise messages are prepared for each participating organization. These may be directions to perform specific tasks, situation information that should be reported, or results for the specific tasks.

e.   **Participant Supplies:** Participants should have available all command and control supplies they would normally use to manage operations. These may include:

(1)   Operational checklists and pre-plans.

(2)   Standard reference books.

(3)   Standard message forms and other emergency management forms.

f.   **Time Required:**

(1)   **Exercise Set-up:** Allow a minimum of one week between providing the initial scenario and exercise instructions and the distribution of the initial messages.

(2)   **Exercise Play:** Allow a minimum of one week for each phase of the exercise.   Depending on the participating agencies, time per phase may be as much as one month, particularly if volunteer agencies that only meet once a month are involved.

g.   **Number Of Personnel Required:**

(1)   **Exercise Controllers:** The exercise may be controlled by a single controller with appropriate secretarial support to prepare and forward exercise elements.

(2)   **Participants:** The number of participants in each agency will depend on how the agency decides to use the exercise. Play can be conducted in three ways:

(a)   To represent the agency in the larger exercise--a single participant would be adequate.

(b)   To train only staff with direct emergency management duties--only those personnel would participate using the scenario as the basis for an internal
143

discussion seminar.

(c)   To train all key staff--the agency may use the exercise to conduct an internal Tabletop Exercise for key staff members.

h.   **Required Facilities:** No facilities are required for exclusive use by exercise participants. Organizations may choose to conduct exercise phases as internal tabletop exercises, using an available conference room, classroom, or their emergency operations center. Exercise control procedures are carried out in a normal office environment by staff of the sponsoring agency.

i.   **Exercise Set-Up:** Exercise controllers prepare a series of files to hold exercise messages received from participating agencies, and set-up a tracking chart to record completion of each phase by each agency.

j.   **Mechanics Of Play:**

(1)   **Group Activity:** Postal Exercises are group activities in which agencies are assigned to emergency tasks they would or could perform in an actual emergency.

(2)   **Time:** Exercise time is phase time based on exercise phases and is not real or compressed time.

(3)   **Phasing:** Because there is a delay in the movement of information due to exchange through the mail medium, a Postal Exercise should be structured in phases. Phasing should be planned as follows:

(a)   Each phase should represent a

specific activity. Phases should be in a logical sequence that mirrors the phases of the type of event that is being simulated.

(b)   Phases should be planned to match with participating organizations' schedules and normal workload. A phase could be conducted each day, several day period, week, or month.

(c)   The number of phases should match the number of desired events or products.

(d)   Not every organization needs to participate in each phase. However, if an agency is not programmed to participate, it may be worthwhile to send a reminder notice and summary of what other organizations are doing to keep the agency informed and involved.

(e)   Documents produced in each phase must have adequate time to flow through normal command, control, and communications channels. As an example of a possible exercise structure, Phase One may be a state agency preparing a disaster warning. In Phase Two the local jurisdictions prepare a damage assessment report based on information provided in the scenario and forward these reports to the state level. In Phase Three the state agency prepares and sends out taskings to resources based on the damage assessments. In Phase Four the resources tasked report when they will be able to respond and what capabilities they will have.

(4)   Sequence Of Events:

(a)   The exercise controller sends each participating agency a basic scenario and exercise ground

145

rules by mail, electronic mail, or facsimile.

(b)   The exercise controller then sends the appropriate participants the first phase problem.

(c)   Participants respond to the exercise controller with their results in the first phase problem.

(d)   The process continues through the subsequent phases until all phases of play have been completed.

(5)   **Output:** Each phase should result in a document that can be sent to a headquarters or a field unit. Examples of such products include written warnings, emergency taskings, situation reports, requests for assistance, damage reports, etc. The document itself may be original, a facsimile copy, or electronic in an electronic mail system.

k.   **Advantages**: Postal exercises are ideally suited for statewide exercises.

(1)   This method forces a tightly focused exercise that addresses a limited number of issues in a standardized way. As a result exercise outcomes are easily measured and evaluated. Furthermore, the performance of each participating organization can be evaluated in comparison with other agencies.

(2)   The exercise format allows agencies that are widely separated to participate in a training event without extensive travel. An entire statewide organization can be exercised at the same time.

(3)   It is significantly less expensive in time,

facilities use and travel costs than many conventional approaches to exercise design.

l. **Limitations:**

(1) Participants tend to feel a lower level of involvement in the exercise, and may assign persons with little experience or decision making responsibility to play the scenario. As a result training value may be less than in face-to-face formats.

(2) Rates of problem return may actually be quite low as agencies may be unwilling to commit any staff time to participation.

(3) Scenarios and problems are rigid and do not easily allow the flexibility of free play exercises.

10.   FORMAL SIMULATION TOOLS:

a. **Description:** A variety of techniques may be used to introduce probable random events and to provide weighted probability or pure chance for event results. These simulation tools provide an exercise less dependent on Exercise Controller judgment.

b. **Level:** Designed for use in exercises at the state and local levels.

c. **How These Tools Are Used:** Simulation Tools may be used in varying degrees to supplement and control play in Floortop Exercises and Postal Exercises. In addition they may be used to design scenario elements for other types of exercises.

d. **Exercise Simulation Tables:** Exercise simulation tables allow exercise controllers to set initial scenario elements randomly and to respond with realistic results to participant actions.

(1) **Scenario Difficulty:** Scenario difficulty can be set by random generator (die roll) or be predetermined by the exercise designer. If determined by die, roll one 4 sided die.

Roll:	Exercise Intensity:	Use These Tables:
1	Low Intensity	Event Month Event Day Of The Week Event Time Of The Day Daylight Or Dark Movement Speed Incident Outcomes
2	Increased Intensity	use the above and add these tables: Basic Weather Conditions Personnel Availability Utility Availability Communications
3	Moderate Intensity	use the above and add these tables: Vehicle Availability Road Blockages Victims Damage To Buildings

4	High Intensity	use the above and add these tables: Alerting Time Changes In Personnel Distractors

(2)   **Random Input Generator:** All random components of the exercise will be generated by use of dice and results tables. Dice used are 4, 6, 8, 10, 12, and 20 sided variants, commonly available from gaming hobby stores. Where possible, 6 sided dice should be distinguishable by having different colors (white, red, blue, green, yellow) to allow more than one computation to be completed at the same time.

(3)   **Event Month:** Some types of disasters may occur only during limited periods during the year. However, for events that may be reasonably expected at any time, roll one 12 sided die to determine the month of the scenario. This table may be modified to use 8, 6, or 4 sided dies for seasonal events.

Roll:	Month:
1	January
2	February
3	March
4	April
5	May
6	June

7	July
8	August
9	September
10	October
11	November
12	December

(4) **Event Day Of The Week:** Roll one 8 sided die to determine the day of the week on which the event occurs.

Roll:	Day:
1	Sunday
2	Monday
3	Tuesday
4	Wednesday
5	Thursday
6	Friday
7	Saturday
8	roll the die a second time

(5) **Event Time Of Day:** Roll one 12 sided die to determine the time of scenario start.

Roll:	Time:
1	0600 (6:00 am)
2	0800 (8:00 am)
3	1000 (10:00 am)
4	1200 (noon)
5	1400 (2:00 pm)
6	1600 (4:00 pm)
7	1800 (6:00 pm)
8	2000 (8:00 pm)
9	2200 (10:00 pm)
10	2400 (midnight)
11	0200 (2:00 am)
12	0400 (4:00 am)

(6)   **Daylight Or Dark:** Based on the month and the time of day established by die roll, operations will start either in daylight or dark based on local average sunrise and sunset for that month. Twilight will extend for 30 minutes before sunrise and 30 minutes after sunset.

(7)   **Alert Time:** Roll one 6 sided die to determine the alerting time for each participating unit. Alerting time includes time to contact the unit and for the unit to alert all available personnel. Two options exist for alerting time tables.

151

The values in these tables may be adjusted based on local statistical data.

(a)   **Staffed Emergency Services Agency And Support Agencies During Weekday Daytime:** These values assume easy alerting of the agency and ability to rapidly mobilize personnel at work.

Roll:	Time Required:
1	1 minute
2	2 minutes
3	3 minutes
4	4 minutes
5	5 minutes
6	6 minutes

(b)   **Agencies Not Staffed:** These values are used for agencies that do not have personnel on duty ready for response.

Roll:	Time Required:
1	15 minutes
2	30 minutes
3	45 minutes
4	60 minutes

5	75 minutes
6	unable to contact the unit - exercise participants may ask that you roll the die a second time after 75 minutes have passed

(8) **Personnel Availability:** Roll one 10 sided die to determine the percentage of personnel available. Paid agency staffing is for the standard work shift. Persons off duty are available at the Volunteer table value rates. This table can be modified to reflect local staffing patterns.

Roll:	Factor X number of Volunteers = Available:	Factor X number of Paid Staff = Available:
1	0.1	0.5
2	0.2	0.6
3	0.3	0.65
4	0.4	0.7
5	0.5	0.75
6	0.6	0.8
7	0.7	0.85
8	0.8	0.9
9	0.9	0.95

0	1	1

To compute personnel available for the scenario take the following steps:

      (a)   Multiply the factor as a decimal value times the number of personnel assigned to the unit.

      (b)   Round up to the next whole person (for example, 0.6 times 9 personnel assigned equals 5.4; round up to 6 personnel available).

      (9)   **Vehicle Availability:** Roll one 10 sided die to determine the percentage of unit vehicles available. This table simulates constraints on the availability of vehicles due to servicing, damage, and other factors which may limit availability.

Roll:	Factor X number of Vehicles = Available
1	0.5
2	0.6
3	0.65
4	0.7
5	0.75
6	0.8
7	0.85

8	0.9
9	0.95
0	1

To compute the number of vehicles available for the scenario take the following steps:

(a)   Multiply the decimal value times the number of vehicles currently assigned to the unit.

(b)   Round up to the next whole vehicle (for example, 0.4 times 7 vehicles assigned equals 2.8; round up to 3 vehicles available).

(c)   Compare number of vehicles with the number of personnel. For volunteer agencies that respond in members' vehicles. the number of vehicles can be no more than the number of people--any value greater than the personnel available is set as the same as the number of personnel.

(10)   **Changes In Personnel:** At the end of the initial operational cycle, deployment period, or duty shift, roll one 8 sided die to determine changes in personnel strength. Do this test for each agency separately, including response resources and command center staffs. This table simulates that differing levels of staffing may be available due to differences in time of day or other emergency commitments.

Roll:	**Total Personnel Change:**
1	lose 1

2	lose 2
3	lose 3
4	no change
5	no change
6	gain 1
7	gain 2
8	gain 3

(11) **Basic Weather Conditions:**

(a) **Cloud Cover And Precipitation:** Roll one 6 sided die at the start of each operational period to determine existing conditions.

Roll:	**Conditions:**
1	clear (sunny if daytime)
2	partly cloudy
3	overcast
4	fog
5	light precipitation
6	heavy precipitation

(b) **Winds:** For all results except fog, roll one 10 sided die and multiply the roll result by 4 to determine wind speed. If wind direction is required for the scenario, roll one 8 sided die to determine direction.

Roll:	Wind Direction:
1	North (360/000 degrees)
2	Northeast (045 degrees)
3	East (090 degrees)
4	Southeast (135 degrees)
5	South (180 degrees)
6	Southwest (225 degrees)
7	West (270 degrees)
8	Northwest (315 degrees)

Note wind direction is the direction from which the wind is blowing and the actual movement of air is the reciprocal value.

(c) **Temperature:** Use the following baseline values for temperatures. They may be modified to reflect historical local temperature values as required.

Season:	Base Temperature:
Winter	30 degrees Fahrenheit
Spring	60 degrees Fahrenheit
Summer	85 degrees Fahrenheit

Fall	60 degrees Fahrenheit

Roll one 8 sided die. Add or subtract the indicated values from the baseline value to determine scenario temperatures.

Roll:	Temperature Change:
1	subtract 5 degrees
2	subtract 10 degrees
3	subtract 15 degrees
4	no change
5	no change
6	add 5 degrees
7	add 10 degrees
8	add 15 degrees

    (12) **Victims:** If the scenario calls for disaster victims to be located, two 6 sided dies are rolled.

    (a) **Victim Condition.** The first die roll determines victim condition.

Roll:			Condition:
A	B	C	
1-2	1		victim uninjured (GREEN)

3	2	1	victim injured - first aid adequate to deal with the problem - evacuation is lowest priority (GREEN)
4	3-4	2-3	victim injured - basic life support or first aid is adequate to sustain the patient - evacuation is required but can be delayed (YELLOW)
5	4-5	4-5	victim severely injured - advanced life support and immediate evacuation required (RED)
6	6	6	deceased (BLACK)

Note that the A Column represents relatively low impact emergency events such as normal traffic accidents, tornadoes, flooding, and open areas in earthquakes. The B and C columns can be used for increased severity of events, and may be modified based on local historical statistical data for major events.

(b) **Victim Accessibility:** The second die roll determines how easily the victim is reached and freed from their predicament.

Roll:	Accessibility:
1	no restriction
2	no restriction

3	victim requires help to walk out
4	victim must be carried out
5	victim is trapped but is easily reached or freed
6	victim is trapped - requires specialized rescue teams

(13)   **Movement Speed:** Sustained movement speeds for long distance movement allowing time for fuel and rest stops with no route blockages are as follows:

Surface:	Speed:
Interstate highways	55 mph
4 lane divided highways	50 mph
4 lane or 2 lane major roads	45 mph
2 lane tertiary roads	40 mph
suburban streets	25 mph
city streets	15 mph
foot movement on road	3 mph
foot movement on trails or across open fields	2 mph
foot movement cross country on hilly terrain, in brush, or open woods	1 mph

(14)   **Road Blockages:** Roll one 10 sided die to test a road or bridge to determine if it is passable. Use this table at specific points in the scenario to inject disaster effects. Do not use these effects for road segments on a regular basis as they have the potential to greatly increase length of playing time.

Roll:	Road Status:
1	no damage
2	no damage
3	passable, but number of lanes reduced by one and speed slowed to: 2 lane road 20 mph 3 lane road 30 mph 4 or more lane road 40 mph
4	passable, but road surface damaged - reduce speed to 15 mph
5	passable, but road structure damaged, partly covered, or partly washed out - reduce speed to 5 mph
6	road blocked by light debris - reduce speed to 1 mph to allow clearing
7	road blocked by heavier debris - one hour delay to clear
8	road impassable - heavy debris
9	road has flowing water across it

0	road washed out or buried

(15) **Damage To Buildings:** Roll one 6 sided die to test damage to buildings.

Roll:	Damage:
1	no damage
2	no damage
3	light damage such as windows blown out or water damage, but building is habitable with minor clean-up and repair
4	moderate damage - building is still structurally sound, but could be used only for emergency shelter after emergency repairs
5	severe damage - building is unusable, uninhabitable, unsafe
6	building collapsed or destroyed

(16) **Utility Availability:** Roll one 6 sided die to test availability of public utilities.

Roll:	Utility:
1	water, power, telephone, cellular telephone available
2	water, power, telephone available

3	water, telephone available
4	water, power available
5	water available
6	no utilities

(17) **Communications:**

(a) **Radio Range:** Communications ranges of field deployed line of sight radio systems are as follows:

Equipment:	Range:
Hand held radio	2 miles
Vehicle mounted radio	6 miles

(b) **Effects Of Terrain:** The following effects are applied to radios based on their deployment.

Situation:	Effect On Range:
Deployed on hill top or other high ground	add 1 mile
Temporary antenna mast erected	add 4 miles
Wooded area	subtract 1 mile

Built up area	subtract 1 mile
Repeater	any station within repeater coverage can talk to any other station in coverage

Specific coverage ranges for specific radio installations can be computed using the standard formula for radio horizon, range equals the square root of antenna height times 1.4.

(c) **Random Effects:** Roll one 8 sided die to introduce random changes in communications capability. These simulate local effects on communications including power line interference, multipath, and differences in line of sight.

Roll:	Change:
1	decrease range 1 mile
2	no change
3	no change
4	increase range 1 mile
5	increase range 2 miles
6	radio batteries exhausted - off the air for ten minutes actual time to change batteries

7	radio ceases operations - can be replaced in 10 minutes actual time if back-up equipment is available
8	interference from an unidentified source causes every other radio message to be garbled so that it cannot be understood

(18) **Random Distractors:** Random distractors may be used to increase the difficulty of the exercise.

(a) **Distractor Frequency:** Roll one 6 sided die to determine the frequency of inputs given as random distractions. Give the next distractor (as determined by the table in subparagraph 2) in the number of minutes indicated below. Roll the die after each distractor to determine the timing of the next distractor.

Roll:	Frequency:
1	3 minutes
2	5 minutes
3	9 minutes
4	13 minutes
5	19 minutes
6	25 minutes

(b) **Distractor Content:** Roll one 20 sided die to determine the distraction event. This list of

165

distractors is a typical example. You should modify the list and add new items on a regular basis so that players don't start to anticipate what problem is coming next.

Roll:	Distractor:
1	Television reporter arrives and wants interview with whoever is in charge.
2	Local elected official arrives and asks for briefing on the situation.
3	One member of your unit complains of feeling sick - he has a fever and vomits.
4	One member of your unit slips, falls, and fractures her forearm.
5	You receive a report that one of your resources will be recalled to deal with another problem (controllers note: the report is not correct and no actual movement of resources will take place).
6	3 civilian volunteers come up to your unit and volunteer to work with you.
7	A local merchant donates three cases of canned sodas directly to the unit - he also wants to donate several cases of beer.
8	Several minor mishaps have occurred and it is obvious that your personnel are becoming tired and a little careless.

9	One agency supervisor is not enforcing rehabilitation for personnel based on physical or psychological condition.
10	You receive a severe weather watch, valid for the next two hours (controller note: insert an appropriate type of severe weather - flash flooding, severe thunderstorm, high winds, tornado).
11	You receive a message for one unit member reference an emergency at home - the member will have to be released to deal with the problem.
12	A local civic club wants to sponsor a barbecue this evening for your personnel.
13	The gas station you have been purchasing fuel from increases prices by 10 cents a gallon.
14	If meals have been requested through support channels, you receive word they will be approximately two hours delayed in reaching your unit.
15	Battery usage has been higher than expected - local stores you check are out.
16	A response vehicle is involved in a minor accident with a civilian vehicle - there are no injuries, and both vehicles sustain minor damage.
17	One vehicle has a flat tire - there will be about an hour delay to fix it.

18	Two personnel are suffering from environmental illness - hypothermia if the weather is colder than 50 degrees and the wind is blowing or there is rain - heat exhaustion if the temperature is greater than 80 degrees.
19	The local jurisdiction Emergency Manager requests a current report of the number personnel and agencies involved in disaster response in his county or city.
20	Request you resubmit your most recent report.

Once a distractor event is used, remove it from the list. If that number is rolled in a die roll, repeat the roll. Once ten events have been used, discontinue use of distractors.

(19) **Incident Outcomes:** To determine whether a specific incident task is successfully completed during a specific phase or hour (of exercise, real, or compressed time) roll one 6 sided die.

Roll:			Results:
A	**B**	**C**	
1-3	1-2	1	Event is successfully controlled. All resources may be released.
4	3	2	Event is partially controlled. Salvage and final clean-up crews only are required.

| 5 | 4-5 | 3-4 | Event is not controlled. Currently assigned resources will be adequate to eventually control it. |
| 6 | 6 | 5-6 | Event is not controlled and is getting worse. Additional resources are needed now to prevent the situation becoming significantly worse. |

Note that A events are minor events, such as a single building fire, that would normally be controlled in one to two hours. B events are major events, such as a hazardous materials spill or multiple building fire, that would normally require from two to six hours for control. C events are catastrophic events, such as a major flood, a major urban fire, or a major terrorist event, that might require six to 24 hours or even days to control.

11.   EXERCISE AFTER ACTION REVIEWS (AAR):

a.   **Description:** An after action review is a formal process designed to perform three critical tasks:

(1)   Identify lessons learned, including both problem areas that require resolution and new, innovative, and successful procedures that should be incorporated or strengthened as standard operating procedures.

(2)   Establish responsibility and a time line for specific actions to incorporate lessons learned.

(3)   Determine future exercise needs.

b. **When Held:** For the types of exercises described in this manual after action reviews should be held as soon as possible after completion of the exercise. This ensures that participants will have the best and most accurate memory of the events of the exercise. The timely after action review helps to reinforce learning. It also provides the best chance of actually getting all the participants to be part of the review.

c. **Format:** After action reviews should include the following topics, conducted as a guided discussion:

(1) Review of exercise objectives.

(2) A brief restatement of key scenario information.

(3) A summary of participant actions in chronological order. This should not be in great detail, but should allow participants to understand what others were doing in the exercise.

(4) Review of procedures and actions that worked well.

(5) Review of procedures and actions that did not work well.

(6) Assignment of items for follow-up.

(7) Determination if exercise objectives were met.

(8) Determination of needs for future exercises.

d.   **After Action Report:** Every exercise should result in a written after action report. This sounds like a lot of work for something as simple as a five minute long Tactical Decision Game. However, you have invested the time to do the exercise; it makes no sense to let the learning that has gone on escape.

(1)   As an absolute minimum the after action report should provide information that you will need to justify or defend the exercise program. This can be done with a one page form filled out by hand or completed on the computer. You must document:

(a)   A very brief description of the exercise scenario.

(b)   The key exercise objectives and whether or not they were met.

(c)   The level of effort required to conduct the exercise - number of participants, staff time required, expenses.

(2)   Adding the lessons learned and the assignments for follow-up will significantly improve the value of the after action report as a tool for exercise program management. It gives you a document you can distribute to all the players to summarize the exercise and encourage follow-up. This also gives you historical data you can review when planning future exercises to determine areas that should be evaluated.

WORKS CITED:

Note to References

In the text Commonwealth of Virginia and United States Government works are referenced by the abbreviations of their agencies as follows:

ARNG   Army National Guard
COVA   Commonwealth of Virginia
DA   Department of the Army
DES   Department of Emergency Services
DH   Department of Health
DMA   Department of Military Affairs
DOT   Department of Transportation
EMI   Emergency Management institute
EPA   Environmental Protection Agency
FEMA   Federal Emergency Management Agency
OEMS   Office of Emergency Medical Services
US   United States
VADF   Virginia Defense Force

Works Cited

Ackerman, John A., publisher of American Fire Journal (8 February 1996), telephone interview by the author.

"Alabama: Command Post Exercise Held." (Summer/Fall 1995). The Journal of the State Guard Association, 4. p. 6.

American Red Cross. Disaster Services Training Support Program (1995). Hurricane Exercise: Virginia. N.p.: American Red Cross.

Antal, John F. (1991). Armor Attacks: The Tank Platoon. Novato, CA: Presidio Press.

_____ (1995). Infantry Combat: The Rifle Platoon. Novato, CA: Presidio Press.

_____ (1998). Combat Team: The Captains' War. Novato, CA: Presidio Press.

Bahme, Charles W. (1978). Fire Officer's Guide to Disaster Control. Boston, MA: National Fire Protection Association.

Benson, Ragnar (1990). Fire, Flash, and Fury: The Greatest Explosions of History. Boulder, CO: Paladin Press.

Brooks, Carol Carlsen (April 1995). "Editorial: Fires, Floods, and Other Catastrophes." American Fire Journal, 46, p. 5.

Brunacini, Alan V. (1985). Fire Command. Quincy, MA: National Fire Protection Association.

Carlson, Gene P. (Ed.) (1983). Incident Command System. Stillwater, OK: Fire Protection Publications.

Cashman, John R. (February 1993). "Hands-on with Haz Mats: The Experts Speak." American Fire Journal, 45, pp. 16-21.

"CEM Degree Rule Reconsidered." (December 1996). NCCEM Bulletin, 13 p. 12.

Central United States Earthquake Consortium (1994). <u>Facilitator Handbook for the Tabletop Exercise to Support The Third National Workshop For Managing Donated Goods And Services held in Charleston, South Carolina, January 28, 1994</u>. N.p.: Central United States Earthquake Consortium.

_____ (1994). <u>Player Handbook for the Tabletop Exercise to Support The Third National Workshop For Managing Donated Goods And Services held in Charleston, South Carolina, January 28, 1994</u>. N.p.: Central United States Earthquake Consortium.

Civil Air Patrol (1992). <u>Training: CAP Operational Missions</u>. CAP Regulation 50-15. Maxwell AFB, AL: Headquarters, Civil Air Patrol.

Cliffside Software, Inc. (1998). <u>Plan AHEAD User's Guide</u>. Portland, OR: Cliffside Software, Inc.

Coleman, Ronny J. (1978). <u>Management of Fire Service Operations</u>. Boston, MA: Breton Publishers.

Collins, Arthur S., Jr. (1978). <u>Common Sense Training: A Working Philosophy For Leaders</u>. San Rafael, CA: Presidio Press.

Commonwealth of Virginia. Department of Emergency Services (1991). <u>Commonwealth of Virginia Emergency Operations Plan</u>. Richmond, VA: Department of Emergency Services.

_____ (1994). <u>Virginia Emergency Operations Center Standard Operating Procedures</u>. Richmond, VA:

Department of Emergency Services.

_____ (1996). Commonwealth of Virginia Emergency Operations Plan. Draft Edition. Richmond, VA: Department of Emergency Services.

Commonwealth of Virginia. Department of Health. Office of Emergency Medical Services (1995). Exercise MEDEX 95: Exercise Plan. Richmond, VA: Virginia Office of Emergency Medical Services.

_____ (1995). Exercise MEDEX 95: Exercise Players Book. Richmond, VA: Virginia Office of Emergency Medical Services.

_____ (1996). Disaster Procedures. Richmond, VA: Virginia Office of Emergency Medical Services.

_____ (1996). Standard Operating Procedures For Virginia EMS Task Forces. Richmond, VA: Virginia Office of Emergency Medical Services.

_____ (1996). Virginia Mass Casualty Incident Management: Module II, Operations Level. Richmond, VA: Virginia Office of Emergency Medical Services.

Commonwealth of Virginia. Department of Military Affairs. Army National Guard (1992). Military Support to Civil Authority for Disaster Response (MSCA-DR). STARC-VA OPLAN 1-92. Richmond, VA: Headquarters, State Area Command - Virginia.

Commonwealth of Virginia. Department of Military Affairs.

Virginia Defense Force (1994). <u>Exercise Warning Order Exercise MAILBAG 1994</u>. Sandston, VA: Virginia Defense Force.

_____ (1995). <u>Warning Order - Exercise MAILBAG 96</u>. Sandston, VA: Virginia Defense Force.

"County News: Cornwall." (Autumn 1994). <u>Civil Protection</u>, p. 15.

Daigle, John, Jr. (August 1996). "Guard Plan Hurries Help." <u>National Guard</u>, pp. 16-18.

Daines, Guy E. (1991). "Planning, training, and exercising." In Thomas E. Drabek and Gerard J. Hoetmer (Eds.), <u>Emergency Management: Principles and Practice for Local Government</u> (pp. 161-200). Washington, DC: International City Management Association.

Davis, Larry (1985). <u>Rural Firefighting Operations: Book One - The first no nonsense guide to Small Community Fire Protection</u>. Ashland, MA: International Society of Fire Service Instructors.

DeVito, James D. (1996). "The Learning Organization." In Robert L. Craig (Ed.), <u>The ASTD Training and Development Handbook</u> (pp. 77-101). New York, NY: McGraw Hill.

Drabek, Thomas E. (1987). <u>The Professional Emergency Manager: Structures and Strategies for Success</u>. Program on Environment and Behavior Monograph 44. Boulder, CO: Institute of Behavioral Science, University of Colorado.

Dunnigan, James F. (1992). The Complete Wargames Handbook: How to Play, Design, and Find Them. New York, NY: Quill.

Eitington, Julius E. (1989). The Winning Trainer. 2nd Edition. Houston, TX: Gulf Publishing Company.

Foster, Harold D. (1980). Disaster Planning: The Preservation of Life and Property. New York, NY: Springer-Verlag.

Front Cover (September/October 1995). 9-1-1 Magazine, 8.

Furey, Barry (June 1986). "Command Post: Sizing Up Hazards With Tabletop Simulation." Firehouse, 11, p. 24.

Greensboro-Guilford County Emergency Management (2000). "A Successful Simulation Event in Guilford County." Available at: http://www.ci.greensboro.nc. us/ema/abbottsville.htm. Accessed 17 February 2000.

Hausrath, Alfred H. (1971). Venture Simulation in War, Business, and Politics. New York, NY: McGraw-Hill Book Company.

Herman, Roger E. (1982). Disaster Planning for Local Government. New York, NY: Universe Books.

Hilburn, Samuel and Richard Parker (1981). Crisis Relocation: America's Halfway Plan for Survival. Eureka Springs, AR: World Survival Publications.

Hoetmer, Gerard J. (1991). "Introduction." In Thomas E. Drabek and Gerard J. Hoetmer (Eds.), Emergency Management: Principles and Practice for Local Government (pp. xvii-xxxiv). Washington, DC: International City Management Association.

House, Ruth Sizemore (1996). "Classroom Instruction." In Robert L. Craig (Ed.), The ASTD Training and Development Handbook (pp 437-452). New York, NY, McGraw Hill.

Illesh, Andrey (1987). Chernobyl: A Russian Journalist's Eyewitness Account. New York, NY: Richardson and Steirman, Inc.

Iott, Richard B., S-3, 4th Military Police Brigade, Ohio Military Reserve (28 December 1995), electronic correspondence with the author.

Joint Commission on the Accreditation of Healthcare Organizations (1995). Comprehensive Accreditation Manual for Hospitals 1995. Chicago, IL: Joint Commission on the Accreditation of Healthcare Organizations.

Kelley, Dennis E. (Fall 1979). "SAR Management Simulator." Search and Rescue Magazine, pp. 8-13.

Knowles, Michael S. and David E. Hartl (1995). "The Adult Learner in the Technical Environment." In Leslie Kelley (Ed.), The ASTD Technical and Skills Training Handbook (pp. 211-241). New York, NY: McGraw-Hill, Inc.

Larson, Randall D. (September/October 1995). "Mobile Command Posts." 9-1-1 Magazine, 8, pp. 38-47.

Linkoping University Hospital. Department of Disaster Medicine (1993). "Emergo-Train System: for education, training and plotting in emergency medical care and rescue services." Advertising brochure. Linkoping, Sweden: Linkoping University Hospital.

MacCrimmon, Kenneth R. and Donald A. Wehrung (1986). Taking Risks: The Management of Uncertainty. New York, NY: The Free Press.

"Maryland: Command Post Exercise Held." (Winter 1994). The Militia Journal, 3, p. 11.

McDaniel, Robert (1996). "Changing Environments: Technology Driven Exercises." The Journal of the American Society of Professional Emergency Planners, 1996, pp. 58-61.

Morentz, James W. (1984). Exercises: A Research Review. Rockville, MD: Research Alternatives, Inc.

_____ (1984). Operating Center Simulations. Rockville, MD: Research Alternatives, Inc.

_____ (1984). Orientation and Tabletop Exercises. Rockville, MD: Research Alternatives, Inc.

National Fire Protection Association (1990). "NFPA 1561 Standard on Fire Department Incident Management System." In 1990 Annual Meeting Technical Committee Reports (pp. 65-87). Quincy, MA:

National Fire Protection Association.

National Voluntary Organizations Active in Disaster
(Summer 1996). "Missouri VOAD Participated In
IEM Course." Newsletter, p. 5.

Nellis, Curt, Chairman, Certified Emergency Manager
Accrediting Commission (13 November 1996),
conversation with the author.

Nordberg, Marie (October 1991). "On the Scene: Lessons
from the Gulf." Emergency Medical Services, 20, pp.
40-61.

Nunnally, Derrick (21 November 1999). "'>Blood,' smoke
give Metro Airport drill virtual reality feel." Available
at: http//library.northernlight.com/PN2000010505000
6915.html?cb=0&sc=0. Accessed 21 February 2000.

Overy, Bob (1993). "The Different Types of Exercise: When
to Use Them." Disaster Management, 5(4), pp. 183-
190.

Pagonis, William G. and Jeffrey L. Cruikshank (1992).
Moving Mountains: Lessons in Leadership and
Logistics from the Gulf War. Boston, MA: Harvard
Business School Press.

Panaction Response International (1996). "Exercise
Overview." Available at: http://www.panact.com.
Accessed 17 August 1996.

Pasquarelli, Tim (9 February 1996 to 8 March 1996), Internet
electronic correspondence with members of the LEPC

Mailing List for LEPC Exercise.

Perla, Peter P. (1990). The Art of Wargaming: A Guide for Professionals and Hobbyists. Annapolis, MD: Naval Institute Press.

Perry, Donald G. (1987). Wildland Firefighting: Fire Behavior, Tactics & Command. Bellflower, CA: Fire Publications, Inc.

Perry, Ronald W. (1991). "Managing disaster response operations." In Thomas E. Drabek and Gerard J. Hoetmer (Eds.), Emergency Management: Principles and Practice for Local Government (pp. xvii-xxxiv). Washington, DC: International City Management Association.

Piskurich, George M. (1993). Self-Directed Learning: A Practical Guide to Design, Development, and Implementation. San Francisco, CA: Jossey-Bass Publishers.

Reed, Wanda, Emergency Medical Services Coordinator, City of Roanoke, VA (1 December 1996), telephone conversation with the author.

Schmitt, John F. (1994). Mastering Tactics: A Tactical Decision Game Workbook. Quantico, VA: Marine Corps Association.

Sebring, Amy (April 1999). "WEBEX: An Experiment in Using Internet Live Chat To Conduct a Functional Exercise." IAEM Bulletin, 16(4), p. 17.

181

Seliger, Jerome S. and Joan Kelley Simoneau (1986). Emergency Preparedness: Disaster Planning for Health Facilities. Rockville, MD: Aspen Publications.

Simonsen, Redmond A. (1977). "Image and System: Graphics and Physical Systems Design." In the Staff of Strategy & Tactics Magazine, Wargame Design: The History, Production, and Use of Conflict Simulation Games (pp. 56-88). New York, NY: Simulations Publications, Inc.

"Skull Session III - No. 40" (April 1989). American Fire Journal 41, pp. 46-47.

"Skull Session III - No. 44" (August 1989). American Fire Journal 41, pp. 44-45.

"Skull Session IV - No. 3" (March 1990). American Fire Journal 42, pp. 54-55.

"Skull Session IV - No. 62" (February 1995). American Fire Journal 46, pp. 40-41.

"Skull Session IV - No. 63" (March 1995). American Fire Journal 46, pp. 26-27.

"Skull Session IV - No. 65" (May 1995). American Fire Journal 47, pp. 26-27.

Smith, August W. (1982). Management Systems: Analyses and Applications. Chicago, IL: The Dryden Press.

Svenson, Raynold A. and Monica J. Rinderer (1992). The Training and Development Strategic Plan Workbook.

Englewood Cliffs, NJ: Prentice Hall, Inc.

The Command Post and MCI Supply (1993). <u>Catalog 93-1</u>.
Milford, OH: The Command Post and MCI Supply.

The Staff of Strategy and Tactics Magazine (1977).
<u>Wargames Design: The History, Production and Use
of Conflict Simulation Games</u>. Strategy and Tactics
Staff Study No. 2. New York, NY: Simulations
Publications Inc.

Tielsch, George P. and Paul M. Whisenand (1979). <u>Fire
Assessment Centers: The New Concept In
Promotional Examinations</u>. Tuscaloosa, AL: Davis
Publishing Company, Inc.

United States. Department of the Army (1984). <u>How
To Conduct Training Exercises</u>. Field Manual 25-4.
Washington, DC: U. S. Government Printing Office.

_____ (1990). <u>Battle Focused Training</u>. Field Manual
25-101. Washington, DC: U. S. Government Printing
Office.

_____ (1993). <u>Domestic Support Operations</u>. Field
Manual 100-19. Washington, DC: U. S. Government
Printing Office.

United States. Environmental Protection Agency (1988).
"Introduction to Exercises in Chemical Emergency
Preparedness Programs." In <u>Guide to Exercises in
Chemical Emergency Preparedness Programs</u> (pp.
1-8) EPA Preparedness and   Prevention Technical
Assistance Bulletin 1. N.p.: United States

Environmental Protection Agency.

United States. Federal Emergency Management Agency
    (1984). Emergency Operating Centers Handbook.
    CPG 1-20. Washington, DC: U. S. Government
    Printing Office.

_____ (1990). Risks and Hazards: A State by State
    Guide. FEMA-196. Washington, DC: U. S.
    Government Printing Office.

_____ (1993). Emergency Management Reporting
    System. FEMA Form 95-44. Washington, DC: U. S.
    Government Printing Office.

_____ (1995). Partnerships in Preparedness: A
    Compendium of Exemplary Practices in Emergency
    Management. Washington, DC: U. S. Government
    Printing Office.

_____ (1997). Partnerships in Preparedness: A
    Compendium of Exemplary Practices in Emergency
    Management. Volume II. Washington, DC: U. S.
    Government Printing Office.

_____ (1998). Partnerships in Preparedness: A
    Compendium of Exemplary Practices in Emergency
    Management. Volume III. Washington, DC: U. S.
    Government Printing Office.

United States. Federal Emergency Management Agency.
    Emergency Management Institute (1987). Exemplary
    Practices in Emergency Management: North Dakota
    "Boys State" Emergency Simulation - A Public-

Private Experience. Monograph Series No. 5.
Washington, DC: U. S. Government Printing Office.

_____ (1989). Exercise Design Course: Guide to
Emergency Management Exercises. SM 170.2.
Washington, DC: U. S. Government Printing Office.

_____ (1989). Exercise Design Course: Student
Workbook. SM 170.1. Washington, DC: U. S.
Government Printing Office.

_____ (1989). The Emergency Program Manager. HS-1.
Washington, DC: U. S. Government Printing Office.

_____ (1990). Introduction to Emergency Management.
SM 230. Washington, DC: U. S. Government
Printing Office.

_____ (1992). Exercise Evaluation Course: Student
Manual. SM 130. Washington, DC: U. S.
Government Printing Office.

_____ (1993). Emergency Operating Center - Incident
Command System Interface Workshop. SM G191.
Washington, DC: U. S. Government Printing Office.

_____ (1995). An Orientation to Community
Disaster Exercises. IS SM 120. Washington,
DC: U. S. Government Printing Office.

_____ (1995). Catalog of Activities 1995-1996.
Washington, DC: U. S. Government Printing Office.

_____ (1995). EOC's Management and Operations

Course. SM 275. Washington, DC: U. S.
Government Printing Office.

_____ (1999). Catalog of Activities 2000. Washington,
DC: U. S. Government Printing Office.

United States. Federal Emergency Management Agency.
Office of Civil Defense (1991). Principal Threats
Facing Communities And Local Emergency
Management Coordinators. FEMA-191.
Washington, DC: U. S. Government Printing Office.

University Corporation for Atmospheric Research (1999).
Community Hurricane Preparedness. Available at:
http://meted.ucar.edu/hurrican/chp/index.htm.
Accessed 19 May 1999.

Vanous, Fred, Emergency Manager, Spotsylvania County,
VA (17 May 1996), personal conversation with the
author.

Washburn, Arthur E., Paul R. LeBlanc, and Rita F. Fahy
(July/August 1994). "Firefighter Fatalities Remained
Low in 1993." NFPA Journal, 88, pp. 55-70.

Wasserman, Ellen (1983). "Simulation exercise in disaster
preparedness training." Disasters, 7(1), pp. 44-47.

Weiss, Raymond A. and M. Gladys Scott (1959).
"Construction of Tests." In M. Gladys Scott (Ed.),
Research Methods in Health, Physical Education,
Recreation (pp. 213-249). Washington, DC:
American Association for Health, Physical Education,
and Recreation.

INDEX

CPSIA information can be obtained at www.ICGtesting.com
Printed in the USA
LVOW041225050612

284306LV00003B/19/A